BEYOND THOUGHT

Yuvraj Sahu

BlueRose ONE.com
Stories Matter
New Delhi • London

BLUEROSE PUBLISHERS
India | U.K.

For permissions requests or inquiries regarding this publication, please contact:

BLUEROSE PUBLISHERS
www.BlueRoseONE.com
info@bluerosepublishers.com
+91 8882 898 898
+4407342408967

ISBN: 978-93-7018-670-5

Cover Design: Aman Sharma
Typesetting: Pooja Sharma

First Edition: April 2025

Preface

What if reality isn't what we think it is? What if everything we see and feel, including ourselves, our world, and everything in between, is an illusion?

For centuries, humanity has tried to define existence. Science helps define the laws and equations of nature while philosophy relates with the questions which science cannot answer.

Philosophy helps to ask questions that science can't. Religion gives faith, purpose, and meaning.

However, even today, we still don't know all truths. Why does consciousness exist? In what ways can belief shape human potential? More importantly, is reality truly as rigid as we assume? Or does it bend? All of this takes us to the past where technology was less advanced?

We as humans have always depended primarily on what we believe. Whether it is religion, an idea, a race, or something else revolutions are started because of beliefs.

But it is not only faith in God or creed that drives us, it is how we interact with the universe. Faith and beliefs decide what is possible and what is impossible. Our beliefs are the limits beyond which we cannot pass.

Belief is the driver of our dreams and fears and the ultimate limits of human beings. What if belief isn't just a psychological phenomenon? What if it's a part of reality?

The contents of this book aren't going to tell you anything you don't already know. This does not replicate old models.

You are invited to question everything.

To face all the assumptions we have that remain unchallenged.

To think whether belief is just something that happens inside us.

Whether it is something that affects existence itself?

Believism is not a religion. It does not replace science or philosophy. Believism supplies a new framework. The one that helps us see reality in a new way. It proposes that, our thoughts, beliefs, and perceptions may influence our world more powerfully than we ever realized. This is not just dreaming or having faith. It is the key that helps you understand the exact nature of reality.

Think about the placebo effect, when believing in a treatment produces physiological changes in the body. A whole society can rise or fall based on the collective belief of the people. Even in quantum physics, looks like what we observe shapes reality at the fundamental level. Coincidence do not exist. Something deeper is suggested here: belief isn't just a passive mental attitude but an active one.

I believe in truth's power, a universal attribute, even if it takes time. Saimon Hill is an author and entrepreneur who has been giving interviews on various topic of Believism. He firmly believes that beliefs create reality. If this is true, what happens when we get skills to control what we believe? When we let go of doubt, fears, and conditioning? This book asks these questions to encourage you to expand your mind through philosophy, psychology, science etc. Also would not answer it all. But it indeed stretches your mind to the limits of possibility.

The idea you most need to put behind you is that reality is fixed, possibilities are limited, and the mind is separate from the world. Think you don't have a say in how your life plays out?

Time to rethink everything.

Welcome to Believism.

Acknowledgements

Acknowledgements

This book wouldn't have been possible without the people who stood by me, inspired me, and challenged me to think beyond the ordinary. First and foremost, I want to thank my family—my mom and dad for their unwavering support, for always encouraging me to explore new ideas, and for believing in me even when my thoughts seemed too unconventional. To my elder brother, for being a guide, a source of wisdom, and someone who constantly pushed me to think deeper.

To my friends and best friends; you know who you are; thanks for all the engaging conversations and debates that shaped many ideas in the book. I truly appreciate your curiosity and skepticism and encouragement.

I would like to thank everyone who took part in my research, those who shared their beliefs. Your words were valuable in developing the ideas in the book. Thanks to all the players I interacted with.

And of course, the publishers and editors who helped realise this vision - thanks for your time and your skills. Your work made this book what it is.

Thank you all for being a part of this.

Contents

Introduction: The Birth of Believism

Introduction

Belief. A word you've certainly heard a million times. "Believe in yourself," they say. "If you believe, you can achieve." Most people regard this as just another motivational saying that we hear and forget in an infinitesimal time-span. But what if belief were more than just a word? What if it were a force; a living, breathing power that shapes not only the reality that we experience each and every day, but also the very core of who we are?

Years back, I remember my dad telling me something very absurd. It was winter, and I was cold. He just looked into my eyes and said, "If you believe that you are not cold, you won't feel it." I laughed at this statement then. How could a mere thought on belief make it happen that one would not feel cold? Yet, many years later, it has caused me to ponder the supposition that he was right.

Suppose that belief is the most potent tool humankind has ever possessed, while we have been too busy overlooking it. Each and every significant advancement over all of history-in science, art, and philosophy-began with someone believing in something that others were as yet unable to see. Every step forward in our private lives begins with the idea that something better can be for us. But belief means not merely thinking well or blind trust-it is an imperative to act. It's aligning your mind and your reality with that which you believe.

Let's analyze it.

The human brain is a marvelous machine. It constantly rewires, adapts, and changes with whatever we think, feel, and go through. This is what scientists know as neuroplasticity. Imagine that your brain is an infinite forest. Every time you have a thought, it makes a path. And as you keep thinking of that thought, you clear and strengthen the path until you can not miss it. And this is how habits form, and how some thought processes-good or bad-are so difficult to break.

"Belief is the final lucial cord on that path." Once you believe in something, your brain doesn't just let go. It starts laying down pathways, connecting your thoughts, emotions, and actions to that belief. This isn't philosophy. This is biology. This is science.

Belief is that intangible but oh-so-powerful mechanism that ushers forth everything from confidence to insanity. It's really proclamation in between knowing and not-knowing; the chasm. Imagine it. Belief is what makes scientists undergo scrutiny-ups to their majestic quarantines-spending years, even decades looking for something that no one else can see. It's what pushes an artist to create something out of nothing. It's what gives kids the guts to take the first steps away from their mother's laps.

Now it gets interesting. Belief is not just individual perspective; it echoes primal to contagion and spreads like rapid wildfire, and it does that because of one utterly devoted believer. This is how movements are made. This is how revolutions are born.

On the other hand, there can also be the darker side. Like faith consolidates, it can fall apart. When you accept yourself for the limitations, your brain creates pathways to solidify that. When you think everyone and everything in the world is against you, you will think you are going to find only problems in the world wherever you look.

Belief is a sign of a reality, hence whether you want it or not; it could be. Well, now here's the question: Are you shaping your reality; or is it shaping you?

This is a book about belief, it tells you what belief is, how it works, why it counts, and how you can harness it in a way that transforms your life. We shall examine the scientific basis of it, some of the ancient wisdom that predicted its power and that has molded history, art, and civilizations.

Now, I'm not here to tell you that "you just have to believe in yourself," or that "you must keep your chin up and cheer yourself on" through hard times. I'm here to push you to question all that you ever thought you knew about belief. Trace it. Dissect it. Think of it not as an interesting idea, but as a force so primal it can change the anatomy of your brain, body, and future.

And so I ask again, what do you believe? About yourself? About the world? Because on the level at which you do, your beliefs are shaping your life-whether you realize it or not.

Chapter 1: The Brain that Believes — The Source of All Realities

Introduction: The Mind as a Creator

What if I told you that your life, with its beams of joy, its curveballs of failure, and its peaks of success, is never truly real? At least not as you have thought. What the mind describes becomes an experience to the person directly linked to it through his/her senses. We have no way of perceiving the realities of our existence–what if your reality is not something you are merely living in but rather the thing you start from?

The human brain fancies itself an architect. A teller of tales. A god in its own right. But this is an eerie revelation: it does not care for the essence of the story; it is only interested in what it makes to you.

Believism begins with one immutable truth: your beliefs are your reality. They are not an influence, not an aftereffect, but rather the point of origin from where the world you live in exists. But don't take this the wrong way; this is not philosophizing in thin air, for we are going to shred it into thin, edible portions until you come to realize that such truth is the most inescapable force in existence.

And now we are left with unveiling the delusion.

1. Belief Is the Lens Through Which You Perceive Reality

Have you ever noticed how no two people seem to leave a situation with the same perception?

Take this example:

Two students arrive late for a class, and the teacher stands with her arms folded in front of the class.

Student A feels quick-witted enough to charm the teacher out of it. They get their first real experience of testing their skill of persuasion.

Student B feels doomed. All they see are punishments and failures.

Same teacher and same conditions, yet two worlds diverge.

What pause it?

Belief. It is not an abstract thought—an unfit filter that reshapes each impression of your life. If you believe the world is against you, you will see evidence for that belief at every turn. Conversely, if you believe the world is full of amazing possibilities, you will find doors where others see only walls.

The world does not happen to you. It happens through you.

Human Connection:

Think back to the last time you were seized by self-doubt. Was it the situation itself that brought you down, or was it the belief that you cannot succeed?

2. The Brain Doesn't Just Observe Reality—It Creates It

Your mind is presumably not a passive interpreter of the world. It constructs, builds, and contorts all things perceived.

Such is the procedure:

The data from the senses-light, sound, touch-come into the brain. But the brain does not passively absorb these sensations. It interprets, fixes, and constructs the reality according to the beliefs.

The Power of Assumptions:

You ever feel your phone vibrate in your pocket, even though you know it actually didn't? That is your brain overwriting reality with expectation.

Now consider: if a belief can override something as simple as sensory input, what else does it modify?

Your identity?

Your potential?

Your understanding of cause and effect?

Thought Experiment:

Close your eyes. Picture yourself achieving everything you've ever wished for. Can you see it clearly? Or does that doubt come creeping in?

That doubt is not real.

It is a belief.

And if one simple thought can obscure your view of success, then what else has it stopped you from seeing?

3. Beliefs Aren't Harmless—They Are Self-Fulfilling Laws

A belief does not just stick inside one head. A belief becomes life itself.

The Loop of Reality:

1. The belief is born.
2. Behavior is led by the belief.
3. Results are produced from the behavior.
4. Results serve further to reinforce the belief.

Hence, the circle continues.

| Example:

A person thinks that he/she is not good at handling social situations.

➞ She runs away from conversations with people.

➞ She finds herself increasingly alone.

➞ The belief sees even deeper roots.

Now let us turn the coin:

A person thinks that he/she is charming.

➞ The person smiles more.

➞ The person strikes up conversations.

➞ The person's social circle widens.

Belief materialized, not because of something true, but because of something believed.

The Scary but Liberating Truth:

If the belief is a dictator over your reality, you are trapped, and you are free. Trapped in that part of the world you never knew you created. But free to change the blueprints for it.

4. The Mind-Body Connection: When Belief Alters Biology

What if belief is something other than just a psychological force? What if belief is a biological force?

Placebo Effect:

Give a patient a sugar pill. Tell them it's a powerful drug. Their bodies start healing as if the pill worked.

Why?

Because they believe it will work.

What about beyond Medicine:

Patients believing they are sick go on to develop physical symptoms.

Patients believing they are strong recover faster from an injury.

If belief can change biological processes down to the molecular level, what else could it control?

Can belief overcome pain?

Can belief slow aging?

Can belief cure otherwise uncurable diseases?

We massively doubt it. It is confronted by this brute invariant of truth.

5. Reality Is Not Objective—It's a Collaboration Between Belief and Perception

Take a moment to pause and reflect on whether reality is actually real.

Perception Is What

Two individuals can be in similar positions yet experience things quite differently. One may see the disaster. The other sees it as an opportunity.

Who is right?

One of them: both.

Because what you call reality is not a solid force outside. It is an agreement on what is there versus what your mind wants you to see.

Truth Is Subjective:

Your consciousness does not give you reality. It gives you merely one version of reality: That version is colored by your history, your apprehensions, and your expectations.

| Relatable Moment:

You misinterpreted someone's tone because you assumed they were upset with you; that is your brain bending reality to conform to its belief.

If belief can reframe something as subtle as a tone, take a look at your whole future.

6. The Roots of Belief: Evolution's Greatest Trick

Belief is not a randomly occurring quirk of human psychology; it is a survival mechanism.

Primitive Humans:

The early humans who felt danger lurked everywhere would outlive those who didn't. Those that took flight upon hearing a rustling bush would survive. Those that thought, "Oh, just the wind" and were wrong would die.

Modern Humans:

We have inherited this instinct. But instead of predation, we project on relationships, careers, and self-representations. The threats come where threats are non-existent.

Reflection:

How many are ghosts carried by mere evolution to haunt you, and how many of your fears emanate from real dangers?

7. The Philosophical Dilemma: Are We Prisoners of Our Own Beliefs?

We ought to meet the chill of an idea that Believism brought forth.

If belief is what builds our world, then Irreality is not universal.

They say it's a matter of perspective.

Freedom Is A Choice:

If the strength of belief does impose upon our world, then changing one's beliefs is not merely an act of oneself.

It is an act of rebellion against the invisible forces controlling your reality.

The Collective Mind:

Entire civilizations are born and die on shared beliefs, nation survives on myths and its' own beliefs push revolutions.

| Deep Thought:

If a belief imprisons us, what has it empowered to free us?

CONCLUSION: THE SEED OF BELIEVISM

Believism is originally not insisting on blind belief; it is the realization that your mind is not passively observing-it is a creator.

A belief is a seed.

It grows into an empire.

The rest are transformed into shackles.

But you are the gardener.

So ask yourself:

What do you believe?

And more importantly...

What will you do to believe tomorrow?

Chapter 2:
The Mechanics of Reality

Introduction: A Universe of Infinite Reflections

If the universe were the mirror, it would not show us one constant truth but rather myriad reflections: all those distorted, amplified, or reduced by some lens through which they are viewed. If reality is a type of shattered mirror, it reflects light but in myriad ways because of the viewpoint of the observer.

The question then comes, if reality itself is not a rigid, objective structure but rather made from countless individual perspectives, then what is truth? How much of what we call real is a fundamental fact, and to what extent is it a function of common agreement, repetition, and belief?

In this chapter, we further develop the fluid nature of reality-with its pattern of breaking down into different versions depending on who looks, what that viewer expects to see, and how their mind processes the given information.

1. The Illusion of Objectivity

Most of us assume that there is an objective reality out there, one world there is belonging to us all, which we all live through in the same way. Evidence has, however, repeatedly suggested the contrary.

Here are two people standing at an intersection of a busy street in a city:

One sees opportunity—flying businesses, stellar architecture, and people moving with purpose.

The other sees decay—pollution, overpopulation, and a system designed to keep people trapped in an endless spiral of struggle.

Are they seeing two different cities? They are not. A person's perception dictates his reality. Moreover, this is not mere psychological slant; neuroscience points some brain functions charged with filtering incoming information, giving priority to whatever aligns with our expectations while virtually disbanding the rest.

Anaïs Nin elaborately quote says this idea:

> ***"We don't see things as they are; we see them as we are."***

If objectivity is the illusion, it follows reality is therefore subjective with unequal premises. In other words, it follows that from different perspectives, even the facts become rather flexible.

2. The Mechanisms of Distortion: How Our Minds Shape Reality

If our experience of the world is constructed rather than merely observed, what factors determine its final shape?

1. Memory—the Unreliable Historian

The past is not recorded like a camera captures footage, it is reconstructed every time we call it to mind. Memories are not fixed; they are written according to our emotions, biases, and our current way of thinking.

This is why two people may go through an event and remember it differently. Studies have shown that eyewitness testimony, often considered among the most reliable forms of evidence, is inaccurate way too often. In this, the mind fills in gaps with false assumptions making reality a rather blurred mixture of that which has actually happened and what we want or expect to have happened.

2. Confirmation Bias—Seeing What We Want to See

Even when someone believes something to be true, he or she will subconsciously be on the lookout for supporting evidence and will dismiss contrary information. Hence two people with opposing political beliefs can view the same debate and each assert that their side won.

Confirmation bias is one of the most virulent forces shaping our personal realities. It builds a self-reinforcing loop: belief leads to selective perception of the belief, which in turn strengthens the belief to the point of making it almost impossible to break out of the loop.

3. The Spotlight Effect—Thinking the World Revolves Around Us

For the most part, we believe we are the center of our world; to some extent, we are. This leads to cognitive distortion in assuming that people notice us and judge us on a greater level than they actually do.

For example, if you trip in public, you might feel embarrassed because you are imagining that every single person around you is taking notice of it and having a laugh at your expense. The truth is that most people are too entrenched in their own little worlds to notice, let alone care.

This knowledge of the phenomenon will set one free. If reality is dependent on attention, then knowing that there is so little attention paid to us by others would free one from unfounded anxiety.

3. The Mandela Effect – When Collective Memory Betrays Reality

One of the most intriguing examples of a large-scale change in reality is The Mandela Effect, named after the common, mistaken belief that Nelson Mandela died in prison in the 1980s, while in fact, he was released and later became the president of South Africa.

Other examples include:

The belief that the Berenstain Bears are really the Berenstein Bears.

The belief that Monopoly's mascot has a monocle (he doesn't).

The belief that *"Luke, I am your father"* can be found in Star Wars (it can't, as the real line is *"No, I am your father."*).

These inaccurate recollections show us that memory is not just a perfect record but also a fluid work in progress. If an entire group of people can assume to remember something in a skewed way, then, more flexible than we take it to be, thinks about the way we view what Reality is.

4. Small choices, Great changes: The butterfly effect.

The reality we live in is shaped not only by perception but also by a trail of events leading up to it. Chaos theory describes The Butterfly Effect, which states that small actions may set off huge domino effects in rather unpredictable ways.

A simple example:

You missed the bus, and therefore you take a different route.

On that route, you meet someone who, years later, becomes your best friend or your business partner.

This relationship leads you to unplayable consequences that could have been completely unpredictable.

At any moment, reality is in bifurcation toward dozens of possibilities radiant from the smallest of choices. If we recognize this, we understand that there actually is no such thing as an insignificant choice.

A wonderful quote from Terry Pratchett about it goes as follows:

> ***"A butterfly flaps it wings in the Amazonian jungle; and, half around the world, a storm arises."***

5. The Echo Chamber Effect - Where Reality Becomes Illusions

In this age of searching and releasing information via social media, the echo-chamber effect refers to a phenomenon where people tend to absorb opinions and information that validate their preexisting beliefs.

This implies:

It fuels confirmation bias.

It gets people to live in mutually exclusive realities.

It causes a cleavage between one set of groups conversing in one version of reality with no symbiotic ground.

If unchecked, this effect makes the reality seem dispersed and truth longitudinally valid instead of axiomatically valid. One could break free of the echo chamber by exposing oneself to contrasting ideas and, more importantly, remaining open to the altering of one's views.

6. The Power of Reframing – Shifting Reality Through Perspective

You'll find the perspective of reflection-an alternative view of reality from the definition of reality as one constructed by perception through the shifting of perception to actually change the reality.

Such things as:

-A failure can be seen as proof of incompetence or as a lesson that builds resilience.

-An obstacle can either act as a hindrance or it can be seen as an opportunity for growth.

-A breakup cannot mean loss or rather new growth.

Well put...as it was said by Shakespeare,

> ***"There is nothing either good or bad, but thinking makes it so."***

This means we wield tremendous power over reality. Through perspective transformation, we turn pain into wisdom, loss into growth opportunity, and chaos into possibility.

7. The Power of the Unseen: How the Subconscious Shapes Reality

Most of the creation of reality takes place under the umbrella of our conscious awareness. The subconscious mind is the silent architect, tirelessly meddling with perceptions, actions, and outcomes. Belief is the blueprint, while the subconscious becomes the builder.

Picture this: if someone is growing up told he is intelligent, hard-working, and capable, his subconscious is going to take it as an absolute truth. As a result, he steps out and displays confidence, takes on challenges, and aims for excellence. Otherwise, if he is constantly told he is worthless or incapable, his subconscious might take in this negativity and subtly sabotage him from excel.

The subconscious never argues; it simply implements the program it has been fed. Hence the reason affirmations, visualizations, and repeated experiences continually mold the reality; they give the subconscious new circuitry and create a refashioning of what is seen as possible.

"The subconscious is the artist painting reality while we merely hold the brush." – Yuvraj Sahu

This invisible force governs:

1. Instincts and Reactions: Our subconscious processes massive amounts of information at hyper-speed and determines how we respond to situations before we consciously even decide.

2. Self-Fulfilling Prophecies: If we just believe something enough, our subconscious makes sure our actions are aligned with making that a reality, good or bad.

3. Dreams and Imagination: Many of our bright ideas and solutions originate from the subconscious mind and act as summons from a space apart from conscious logic.

To take charge of reality, the art of subconscious reprogramming has to be learnt and accomplished. This is not an easy ask, but through repetition, consciousness, and intention, it can be refashioned to one's advantage.

8. The Role of Language in Constructing Reality

Language Forms Reality

Words are in more than one way a pattern of reality construction. The language we use shapes our perception, and in turn, perception becomes the root for our actions.

"Every spoken word is a seed planted in the garden of reality." – Yuvraj Sahu

By continuously repeating the expression "I am unlucky," people eventually condition their minds to perceive only misfortunes, thus realizing their own beliefs about unfortunate occurrences. However, those who are more prone to say, "I make my luck" would be more willing to face risks, look out for chances, and consequently build something on positive outcomes.

The Sapir-Whorf hypothesis suggests that language works not only as a reflection of reality; it also shapes reality. In cultures that do not have a word for "impossible," people achieve things others believe to be impossible. Language creates the framework within which our beliefs enact.

To this end:

Positive language promotes empowering beliefs ("I am able," "I shall find the way").

Negative language reinforces limiting beliefs ("I cannot do this," "This is too difficult").

The words we listen to affect us as much as the words we utter.

Being careful with our language means creating a version of reality that envies the other one, one sentence at a time.

9. The Reality of Time: Linear vs. Perceived

We often think of time as a strict sequence, a linear flow from past to future. This is only one way to perceive it. An action in the past affects the immediate present. Real time travels, in a more intangible sense-created by belief and perception.

Have you ever noticed how time slows down when you are bored but flies by when you are engaged? This is not an illusion; rather it is perception altering experience. Athletes talk about the flow state where time seems to stretch or compress as necessary. In danger, people often remember experiencing time in slow motion.

"Time is not measured by clocks but by moments." -Yuvraj Sahu

It questions if reality is strictly bound by chronological advance. If time is elastic, influenced by perception, then from a perception standpoint, one has control over time.

By changing focus and immersing oneself in the present moment, we can "slow down" time so that experiences become richer and fuller. Likewise, by anticipating future success with conviction, we pull that future closer to our present reality.

10. The Collective Illusion of Reality

Much of what we call "real" is just a consensus reached by humanity. Money has value because we all agree it has value. Borders exist because nations recognize their values. Titles, rules, and traditions hold up because society, as a collective, holds them up.

"The greatest illusion is that reality is fixed; the greatest power is knowing it isn't." -Yuvraj Sahu

It means that in order to change the reality, you may not necessarily need to fight against it, and most of the time you would just need to replace the collective belief. Social movements, revolutions, and paradigm shifts occur.

11. The Fine Line Between Delusion and Vision

Both dreamers and delusional people choose to believe in things no one else can see; the difference lies in the execution.

A visionary creates a new reality in spite of opposition; a delusional person ignores the reality and stubbornly sticks to an unchangeable point of view.

"A belief without an act is merely a wish; a belief with an act is a reality yet to unfold." - Yuvraj Sahu.

The history is filled with the names of such people who seemed deluded:

The Wright brothers: "Man will never fly."

Nikola Tesla: "Wireless electricity is nonsense."

Marie Curie: "Women in science? Impossible."

They were considered insane until their beliefs began to reshape reality itself. This is a lesson in which we can learn the world does not undergo change merely through passive observation but acting belief coupled with effort.

To determine whether one's belief is a vision or delusion, ask:

Can this be achieved with effort and adaptation?

Is there evidence to hold this possible?

Am I willing to adjust according to the new reality?

If yes, then what others call impossible, is in fact, simply a forthcoming reality.

12. The Paradox of Certainty: Does Reality Demand Absolute Truth?

In all likelihood, we are wired to seek certainty, yet reality itself is not static. Throughout history, man has clung to the "absolute truths," all of which have by now been totally dismantled. What today passes for knowledge may tomorrow be looked on as primitive.

"Certainty is an illusion we cling to against an unpredictable universe to derive comfort from it." –Yuvraj Sahu

Listen to why scientific revolutions:

When Newton spoke of the final word about motion, Einstein's relativism was not in vogue.

Classical physics ruled until quantum mechanics opened up a new, stranger reality.

Germ theory nabbed the thrones once occupied by bad air.

Thus, these changes show that reality does not depend on absolute truth but, instead, reality stems from one's own growing understanding. As soon as something is laid with the stamp of "unchangeable fact," that constricts the mind toward any further possibility.

In such a paradox, the future would take shape as those pliable to new interpretations, new discoveries, & new perspectives. Accepting a reality perpetually in flux liberates from the shackles of dated beliefs.

13. The Energy of Belief: Can Thoughts Shape Physical Reality?

Research in psychology suggests that people are affected in their health, rate of recovery, and performance through ways in which they think. Physics studies suggest that consciousness plays a role in shaping matter.

"The universe does not ask If your belief is logical; it simply aligns with the energy you emit." – Yuvraj Sahu

An idea that used to be dismissed as pseudoscience is brought to the label of experiment by physics and neuroscience. Observation can alter quantum particles. Can the belief of man alter reality?

Mechanisms may be unclear, but the trend is undeniable:

Those who visualize success tend to perform better.

Willing patients heal faster.

Optimistic live longer.

Reality is not merely being; it is reactive. The question is not whether or not belief influences reality, but to what extent it does.

14. Quantum Entanglement: Observers and the Uncertainty of Reality

Quantum mechanics suggest that quantum particles exist in any one of the possible states until the time there is an observation done. It essentially tells us that core reality is determined by interaction.

"The universe is a question waiting for an observer to answer." – Yuvraj Sahu

This leads to deeper unanswered questions:

Does reality exist itself, or is it defined at the very moment of interaction?

If observation modifies existence, how far does our power reach?

Can the human mind really be entangled with reality in a basic sense?

Science has not much provided a grounding. However, the consequences, mind-boggling. If reality is altered by virtue of interaction, control over perception is not mere psychological gimmick but instead a potent force.

15. The Role of Chaos in Reality's Design

Many distrust chaos, but what if that chaos is not the enemy of order but instead serves as the womb for birthed realities?

"Chaos is where new realities are formed." – Yuvraj Sahu

Think of history's most chaotic moments:

The fall of Rome ushered in the Renaissance.

The destruction of old industries brought about technology revolutions.

Personal crises lead almost invariably to a breakthrough that may change one's life.

Reality is never a straight path; it is a storm in the making. Any resistance toward chaos is a resistance toward transformation. Those who accept it, however, do not simply endure change; they orchestrate it.

16. Final Reflection: What Reality Will You Create?

The question is not one of whether reality is fixed or fluid; rather, one of whether reality is witnessed or characterized as observed or subjectively felt. In truth, the real question here is:

How do you wish to interact with reality?

Reality is both a stage and a script, both a playground and a puzzle. It is neither entirely written nor entirely blank-it is an open-ended story just waiting for new authors to shape it.

"Reality is not something that you watch; it is something that you create."-Yuvraj Sahu.

We have always possessed the power to make reality. It lies most fully in the beliefs we have, perceptions we hold, and where we choose to direct our attention.

What, then, will you say?

Chapter 3: The Neuroplasticity of Belief — Rewiring Reality

Introduction: Your Brain, Your Blueprint

Picture an artist skillfully shaping a block of clay. In this analogy, your brain represents the clay while your beliefs serve as the artist's hands. Every thought you entertain, each experience you encounter, and every repetition acts to sculpt your neural pathways, solidifying how you perceive reality.

For many years, it was widely accepted that the brain ceased to change after childhood–viewed as a rigid organ inevitably heading toward decay with age. However, recent advances in neuroscience have dismantled this conventional belief. The brain is far from being a static instrument; it is a dynamic and adaptable organism capable of reshaping itself throughout one's life.

This phenomenon is known as neuroplasticity–it demonstrates that belief transcends mere cognitive thinking; it functions as a tangible force. Our beliefs actively modify our brain structure, guide our decision-making processes, and determine our experiences within reality.

In this chapter, we will examine:

- The underlying science of neuroplasticity which illustrates the potency of belief

- How constraining beliefs develop and can entrap individuals in patterns of failure

- Techniques to reconfigure your mindset for achieving success, fulfillment, and boundless potential

- The interplay between neuroplasticity, physical health, and genetic factors

Understanding these concepts goes beyond intellectual knowledge about the brain; it revolves around regaining authority over both your mind and future direction.

This is more than just understanding the brain. This is about reclaiming control over your mind and future.

What Is Neuroplasticity?

Neuroplasticity refers to the brain's remarkable capability to adapt, reconfigure, and evolve in response to various experiences, thoughts, and behaviors.

The term can be broken down as follows:

- **Neuro**: Pertaining to neurons (the cells of the brain)

- **Plasticity**: The capacity for being molded or reshaped

Imagine your brain as a network of highways. Each road represents neural pathways that connect different areas of the brain. When you frequently travel along a particular route, that path becomes more robust and easier to navigate. Conversely, when you cease using a specific pathway, it gradually weakens and may ultimately fade away.

This dynamic is mirrored in how beliefs are formed:

Reinforcing a belief consistently strengthens it; however, if reinforcement ceases, the belief diminishes over time and may eventually vanish.

Types of Neuroplasticity

Neuroplasticity manifests in two primary forms:

1. **Structural Neuroplasticity** – This involves physical alterations within the brain's structure such as the formation of new neurons or the elimination of old connections.

2. **Functional Neuroplasticity** – This aspect allows for shifting functions from damaged regions of the brain to healthier ones.

Both processes underscore an essential truth about your brain: it is not static but rather continually changing. Every thought, belief, and action contributes physically to rearranging your brain's circuitry.

How Beliefs Influence Brain Function

Beliefs are not mere abstract ideas; they serve as biological frameworks that influence neuron connections and communication.

Recent research in neuroscience indicates that beliefs can fundamentally reshape the brain, following several key principles:

1. Neurons That Fire Together, Wire Together

Whenever you engage in thought or action, certain neurons activate simultaneously within your brain. The more frequently these neurons fire together, the stronger their interconnection becomes.

For instance:

If you repeatedly convince yourself that “I am inadequate at public speaking,” the neuronal pathways linked to anxiety and a sense of failure will become reinforced.

Conversely, when you begin affirming to yourself “I am confident and capable,” new neural pathways emerge. Over time, this fosters a state where confidence is your natural response.

2. The Emotional Component

Emotions function as the connective tissue for neural pathways. When beliefs are associated with intense emotions, they tend to become firmly embedded in your brain structure.

Beliefs rooted in fear (for example, "I will never achieve success") create robust and enduring neural circuits that make experiences of failure feel almost predetermined.

On the other hand, positive beliefs (such as "I possess the ability to tackle challenges") stimulate the brain's reward system, which enhances motivation and promotes resilience.

3. The Importance of Repetition

The human brain seeks efficiency above all else. If a belief is repeated sufficiently, it becomes ingrained into subconscious thought processes.

Daily reinforcement of negative thoughts can lead them to dominate your mindset by default.

By consistently practicing positive affirmations each day, you can effectively reprogram your subconscious identity.

This underscores why techniques such as self-affirmations, visualization exercises, and habit formation prove beneficial—they leverage neuroplasticity to cultivate new belief systems.

The Impact of Limiting Beliefs on Mental Cycles

Limiting beliefs function as self-created obstacles. They become ingrained within your neural pathways, causing feelings of failure and self-doubt to arise automatically.

These beliefs typically stem from:

Childhood Conditioning – When a child frequently hears phrases like, "You aren't smart," the mind often adopts that perspective as truth.

Negative Experiences – Encounters with failure, trauma, or critical remarks solidify pathways associated with self-doubt.

Social Influence – Cultural norms and societal expectations shape our understanding of what is achievable or unattainable.

The Formation of Limiting Beliefs in the Brain

Picture a river gradually eroding a canyon through rock.

With each passing moment (negative thoughts), the channel deepens (belief).

As this channel becomes deeper, altering the flow of the water (thought) becomes increasingly challenging.

This illustrates why persistent negative beliefs seem so resilient—they are embedded within our neural structure. Nevertheless, neuroplasticity provides an opportunity to forge new pathways, enabling you to redirect your thought processes toward achievement and positivity.

Breaking Free: How to Rewire Your Brain for Success

Rewiring your mind is a deliberate process that necessitates focused effort, adhering to a clear and systematic approach:

1. Awareness: Recognize Limiting Beliefs

Transformation begins with self-awareness; you cannot alter what remains hidden. The first task is to pinpoint the limiting beliefs that impede your progress.

Consider these questions:

- What negative thoughts do I find myself repeating on a daily basis?

- Where did these beliefs originate from?

- Are these beliefs unchangeable truths or mere viewpoints?

2. Challenge the Belief

Questioning an existing belief diminishes its established neural pathways.

Rather than thinking, “I’ll never achieve success,” formulate instead: “What evidence supports my potential for success?”

Instead of saying, “I’m not good at this,” ask yourself: “Have I truly given myself the opportunity to improve?”

3. Formulate New Beliefs

Upon exposure of a limiting belief, it must be substituted with an affirming one.

For instance:

- Transform "I am not a skilled public speaker" into "I enhance my skills with every attempt.”

- Change "I always fail" to "Failure provides essential feedback that helps me grow."

4. Reinforce Through Practice

Repeatedly affirming your new beliefs strengthens synapses in the brain.

Methods for reinforcing beliefs include:

- **Affirmations** – Articulate your newfound belief on a daily basis.

- **Visualization** – Envision yourself achieving your goals successfully.

- **Physical Action** – Take small yet purposeful steps that resonate with the new belief.

5. Attach Positive Emotion

Emotion enhances neuroplasticity significantly. By associating feelings of excitement, confidence, or gratitude with new beliefs, you expedite their integration into your mindset.

The Mind-Body Connection: Beyond the Brain

Beliefs do not only influence thoughts; they affect your entire body:

Placebo Effect – The belief in healing can have real biological recovery effects.

Psychosomatic Illness – Stress and negative thinking manifests in physical disease.

Epigenetics – Long-term beliefs influence the expression of genes and can even affect your future generation.

By changing your beliefs, you are essentially rewiring your biology.

Methods to Enhance Neuroplasticity

To accelerate the rewiring of your brain, consider incorporating these strategies:

1. **Meditation** – Enhances concentration and promotes self-awareness.

2. **Journaling** – Aids in breaking patterns of negative thinking.

3. **Physical Activity** – Encourages the release of chemicals that facilitate neural restructuring.

4. **Acquiring New Skills** – Fosters greater cognitive adaptability.

Neuroplasticity in Everyday Life: Evidence That Belief Influences Reality

The concept of belief-driven neuroplasticity transcends theory; it is reflected in tangible real-life instances where individuals have transformed their circumstances through mental reprogramming.

Case Study 1: The Stroke Survivor Who Rehabilitated His Brain

Dr. Paul Bach-y-Rita, a prominent neuroscientist, conducted extensive research on stroke survivors who had lost certain motor functions but subsequently regained mobility by engaging in mental exercises. One particular patient experienced paralysis yet dedicated time each day to visualize movement.

Over an extended period, his brain adapted, reallocating motor functions to unaffected regions.

This case illustrates how consistent belief and determination can help overcome formidable physical challenges.

Case Study 2: The Efficacy of Placebo in Recovery

Research from Harvard revealed that patients assigned sugar pills branded as "powerful painkillers" reported notable relief from their ailments—even though they received a placebo treatment.

What accounted for this phenomenon? Their strong belief triggered the body's natural pain-relieving mechanisms (endorphins).

This serves as compelling evidence that belief has the ability to bring about physiological change.

Case Study 3: The Athlete Who Primed His Mind for Achievement

A renowned Olympic study observed two groups of skiers:

1. One group underwent physical training.
2. The other solely visualized successful skiing performances.

Upon evaluation, both teams demonstrated comparable improvements in performance levels.

The visualization group was able to fortify their neural pathways without any actual practice involved.

This confirms that mental conditioning can effectively rewire the brain just like physical activity does.

These examples affirm that belief is not merely subjective—it wields significant neurological power and influence.

Why Changing Beliefs Feels Difficult (And How to Overcome It)

There are many reasons for which people feel that while changing or reframing their beliefs is very important, they find themselves not able to deal with this very task.

The three main problems:

1. The Brain Balks at Change:

Your brain was built to work efficiently rather than to change. After several years of inducting a belief, your brain may resort to it in order to be energy-efficient.

Overcoming Strategy:

1. Start with small changes; small shifts compound into huge changes.

2. Add new beliefs to preexisting routines (such as affirmations while brushing your teeth).

2. Fear of Identity Loss:

Truth is that beliefs are one of the core features that often define your identity. Changing those would feel as if you're erasing part of yourself.

For example: If all along you believed that you are not good at any relationship, the idea of succeeding at this may fall away.

Overcoming Strategy:

Think of yourself as adaptable: "I am always changing and evolving."

Shift your focus from perfectionism to growth; belief changes take time.

Once you overcome the above roadblocks, you will have no idea how to hold back on belief rewiring anymore.

Chapter 4: The Science of Neuroplasticity

Advanced Techniques to Rewire Beliefs Faster

To elevate neuroplasticity, here are advanced techniques that turbocharge belief transformation.

1. The "As If" Principle

The brain doesn't recognize the distinction between real experiences and imagined ones.

Instead of waiting for proof, act as if the new belief is already taut.

Example: If you desire confidence, walk, talk, and think like a confident person-NOW.

The neurons begin rewiring instantaneously when you live as if the belief were already real.

2. Cognitive Reframing Method

This method is to find alternative explanations for the failures of the past.

Example:

Instead of thinking "I failed because I am not smart."

Reframe into "I failed because I didn't have the right strategy, and now I know how."

Why it works:

Your brain actually makes new connections, based on the reframed ideas.

3. Time-Based Neural Conditioning

It is scientifically proven that the brain actually solidifies beliefs during deep sleep and early morning states.

Textarea new beliefs just before sleep and after waking, or visualize successes to most efficiently tie new beliefs into your subconscious.

4. The "Contrast Shock" Method

Intense, contrasting experiences teach the brain well.

If public speaking gives you constant fear, you should expose yourself to massive controlled stress by volunteering for an event.

The shock destroys the beleaguered brain circuitry and forces it to realign.

This method rapidly rewires fear-based beliefs into confidence.

Final Statement: Your belief is your superpower.

Most people have been conditioned to identify with beliefs, but that's an illusion of the mind.

Your beliefs are not facts; they're merely repeated neural patterns that can be changed any moment.

You are the observer, not the belief.

If a belief doesn't serve you, simply overwrite it.

Science affirms what philosophers have said for centuries:

What you believe makes you.

Your brain is pliable, adaptable, and without limits.

Neuroplasticity proves you're not a mere plaything of the universe; you're the architect of your own mind.

And so the question lingers: "What will you choose to believe?"

Chapter 5:
The Laws of Believism

> "Your beliefs do not shape your world; your world-shaping beliefs shape the world."

Not just believing; it'd be about how belief interacts with reality; belief is like a string of programming code that runs the system called your life. If you write faulty code (beliefs-both weak-limiting), your system called life will not run the way you envisioned. But if you program in the right way (strong-empowering beliefs), then you can create whatever reality you wish.

There are laws that govern this belief, which if understood, give all the benefits of the universe. These laws are not about wishing things come true; they are about controlling the forces that make reality. If you have ever wondered why some people are considered lucky while others keep struggling, they would lay their sword on the ground in these laws.

If you Hither, to master them, this world will not be a puzzle anymore but a tool.

Law of Intention: "You Become What You Focus On"

> Both sharp and dull blades cannot cut equally and easily through a piece of wood. The same is true with the mind.

The mind is a focusing instance! Wherever you put your attention, energy flows. Consider two people standing in the rain. One is cursing the rainstorm because it is a miserable inconvenience. The other is dancing; the lovely fresh air and cool drops feel divine. The same rain, yet two absolute extremes of experience! Why? Because focus differs.

Whatever you will focus on, it will become your reality. Think all the time about failing, and these thoughts will influence your actions. If you are prone to dreaming of success, then the opposite happens. This is why dreamers who never act remain dreamers, while doers remain achievers.

A warrior who enters the battlefield believing he has already been defeated will hesitate; thus, defeat is inevitable. But a warrior who enters with confidence, picturing himself as winning, steers and aims with precision-thus making victory that much more likely.

How will you put this into practice? Write down what you want. Wish on no prospects, fear no scenarios that will seem bad: instead, go for something you genuinely wish for. Then just write down what thoughts, actions, and feelings you are channeling toward that goal every single day.

The Law of Belief: "What You Believe, You Become"

> ***"A prisoner who believes they are free will look for an escape. A free man who believes he is trapped will never leave his cage."***

If you could take two identical people and install opposite beliefs in them, their lives would take completely different paths: one would rise to success while the other would remain stagnant–and, indeed, all due to one's internal programming.

Take a street performer who plays the guitar for money. One could say to himself, "I'm just a beggar that plays this instrument." Another might convince himself, "I am a future rockstar-in-training." The first might play with extreme embarrassment, counting the pennies on his hat. The second would play with passion and draw a growing crowd with his outstanding musical prowess.

Same action, different beliefs—completely different outcomes.

Application: Check every belief you have about yourself: is it supporting you or limiting you? If the latter, destroy it! Replace it with one that empowers you.

The Law of Action: "Action Reinforces Belief"

> ***"A lion that never hunts forgets it is a hunter."***

You can't think your way toward confidence. You have to act your way toward confidence. This law states that belief blossoms through action. If you want to conquer fear, do your small overcoming fear actions. If you want to become an experienced practitioner, train until excellence becomes instinctive.

A training swordsman believes himself weak. But if he picks the sword and carries on training every day, that belief will soon change. The more he engages in action, the more his confidence builds. He no longer believes he is strong; he knows he is strong.

This is why it is only through action that doubt can be dismantled. Feeling incapable? Take action. Even the tiniest step makes it clear in your own mind that you are not as weak as you think.

Application: Do something today which is consistent with your desired belief. Make it small if you want. That will only serve to solidify the foundation you have laid to validate your self-image.

The Law of Perception: "What You Perceive is What You Experience"

> "A traveler who believes that every road is dangerous will never see the beauty of the journey."

The nature of reality itself is subjective; it is filtered through perception. One person raised in hardship may perceive the world as cruel and another in love may perceive it to be kind; the world never changed, just their perceptions.

A farmer looks at the storm and panics about his crops being spoiled; a sailor observes that storm and welcomes strong winds in an effort to expedite his travel. It is never the event, rather it is the perception of the event that determines experience.

Application: When you meet a challenge, ask yourself: Can I look at this differently? Change your perception, and you will change your reality.

The Law of Consistency: "Show Up, Come What May"

> "It is not strength that carves the river into stone. It is relentless persistence."

Constant alteration has become the greatest enemy of success. Things are often started with excitement but abandoned if results start to come late in the day. According to this law, perfection and change are ultimately achieved only via sustained constancy.

A knight is not made by one short training. A musician is not built merely on the basis of a one-time performance. Real strength is built upon repeated practice.

It is the people who refused to give up that rose to stardom. All great craftspeople were once an amateur until consistency makes them a master.

Application: Set a goal and commit to it every day, regardless if the motivation fades. This is your time to become successful while no one is watching.

The Law of Alignment: When mind, action, and belief operate together, the world takes a turn.

> ***"A warrior who doubts fights without knowing, and a warrior who believes has a considerate force. But the one who aligns mind, body, and spirit? He is unstoppable."***

When the belief, the mind, and the action are harmonious, this is called alignment. Once you hit alignment, life flows freely.

A musician can think, "I am a world-class guitarist." And, he thinks that every mistake he makes is progress while he practices every day. Success is just a result of this.

But the moment he gets a thought of his failure, there is a shadow that pervades his thought, and he will only take actions with doubts. Ultimately, this affects his progress.

Application: Ask: Are my beliefs, thoughts, and actions working with each other or against each other? If anything is working against them, correct it.

The Law of Gratitude: "Appreciation Multiplies Abundance"

> ***"A king who is never satisfied will always feel poor. A beggar who appreciates life will feel like a king."***

Gratitude is the incantation that adds to and amplifies everything. In whatever you give gratitude, you shall receive in more abundance. If your focus is on what you lack, you shall forever feel incomplete. If your focus is on that which you have, you shall create and live in abundance.

A grateful man wields the power over talent, becoming a fast learner. To appreciate one's opportunities opens many doors.

Apply this: Give gratitude for at least one thing every day. Notice how it changes your thoughts and energy.

The Law of Persistence: "Keep going no matter what."

> "Storm tests the tree, but he who stands strongest is he who deepens his roots."

Every path has obstacles. The difference between success and failure is the person who continues and the person who dares not. Only those who quit never achieve their objectives.

There are times when every hero stands poised to give up; but to those who stand firm, who refuse to yield- there lie the legends.

Application: Whenever you encounter failure, tell yourself: This is not the end. This is just a passing test. Conquer it, and you'll have risen stronger.

Conclusion: The Path Forward

The laws of Believism are not mere ideas; they are the very forces of reality. They work whether one wants to acknowledge it or not-Is gravity acknowledged by one and all? The success of certain individuals and the failure of others are absolutely by the laws that one understands and applies to one's.

With knowledge, you are no longer a slave to circumstance. You can create your destiny. The universe, the reality at large, does not resist the will of the doers of great beliefs-it bends to it.

Yet belief alone is not enough. Empty lies the knowledge, unto the actions there are none. Empty understanding. Hence, go ahead-human mind and belief systems are put together-give your actions focus. Do not take no for an answer.

You create your reality, and the only question left is:

Will you create it, or will you allow it to create you?

Chapter 6: Fear and Belief: Two Sides of the Same Coin

While fear and belief appear to be disparate opposites, they're actually much more related than one would ordinarily imagine. These outflows emanate from the mind, an infinite power of imagination, a creativity and manifestation power combined. Fear and belief hold two inheritances through the coin, the former being able to form a reality and do the things that are unable to be done otherwise.

Believe and fear are still intermingled: a journey into how fear may inhibit or drive you forward and how belief forms the antidote which transmutes fear to strength.

Paradox of belief and fear

Fear really is the belief II that something is around; really wrong. Belief is empowering; fear is only a weakness, confinement. In fact, the most primal force for fear and belief originates in entrusting-the whole dreaming of tomorrow not yet come into some kind of actual reality.

The paradox is a truth about an idea, in that you take the risk energy and what could be and transform it into belief. In simpler terms, fear is wrong imagination. Confront this energy, and the weakest part of your armor becomes your strongest weapon.

Observe a child learning to ride a bicycle. The child is afraid it will fall because of its belief-not because it will fall. The key moment happens when the child rides alone with its will for the first time and shifts from believing it will fall to believing it can ride the bicycle.

Fear congealed into belief: the energy of possibility in the form of belief. Once established, the fear is no more a master; it practically becomes a servant before the belief systems.

The Nature of Fear: A Shadow of Possibility

Fear is certainly present in the unknown. It is but the shadow haunting you in the spotlight of other possible realities. But here's where it gets quite interesting, you see: fear only appears when you're on the verge of going into uncharted lands; it has never been there when you do feel comfortable. The moment you are about to step forward or intend to step up is when fear steps in.

Have you ever known the fear of giving an important speech, of competing, or of doing something totally new? Such fear should stand as a real gesture that soon, you would transcend the limits you have confined yourself to. Unless you are stuck and there is no chance at all that you are in danger, you are not in the fear; fear is only present on the threshold of growth.

Upon feeling fear, ask yourself: What shall I learn from it?

Fear is merely a reflection on self-growth and affirmation of self-belief.

Some examples include:

The fear of failure → Build upon self-belief in order to learn and adapt.

The fear of rejection → Derive self-worth from inner validation, and never let external affirmation govern you.

The fear of uncertainty → Establish firm faith in your ability to change.

Fear is a signal, not a stop sign. It is an indication that you must strengthen your belief.

The Power of Belief Over Fear

Belief does not eliminate fear; it overrides it.

If fear is a dark room, then belief is the light switch. With the presence of belief, darkness (fear) has no choice but to recede. This is the most basic truth of the mind: whatever you focus on expands.

The moment you give your attention to fear, it becomes more powerful. The moment you give your attention to belief, it gets more strengthened.

Courage to take action comes from belief despite fear. It reminds one that, though fear could be transitory, rewards for taking a leap of faith will remain.

The big achievers in the world are not fearless. They are simply masters of belief. They experience fear but choose to associate with belief. They hear doubt but act indeed.

Example: The plunging person at the edge of the diving board is filled with fear. However, if the belief in their ability to jump correctly is right in that moment, they leap. In that moment, the fear is there, but belief guides them forward.

Fear is an instinct and belief is a decision. The question now is: which instinct do you allow to control your actions?

How Fear and Belief Interact

Fear and belief are always engaged in conflict.

In cases where fear becomes dominant, belief is weakened.

When belief becomes justifiably strong, fear loses its power to speak.

Don't treat this relationship as a war, it's just an equilibrium to be mastered. Fear can be a good thing when you observe it with detachment.

Fear must be treated not as a deterrent but as a navigation tool. It outlines the points in your belief that remain unexplored.

For example:

Fear of public speaking?→Build belief in your voice.

Fear of failing in the driving test?→Build belief in your preparation.

Fear of being alone?→Build belief in your self-worth.

Fear is like an alarm ringing inside your mind. The question is, would you let the alarm paralyze you or wake you up?

To overcome your fears: A step-by-step guide

1. Identify: Acknowledge and accept that you are feeling fearful. Clarity is a crucial first step in overcoming fear.

2. Question: Ask yourself: Is this a reality-based fear or an assumptive one?

3. Change: Trade frightening thoughts with affirmations grounded in belief.

4. Act: Taking even the smallest step diminishes fear.

5. Reflect & Grow: After you have faced a fear, ask questions such as: What have I learned? How has this strengthened my belief?

Each encounter with fear is a victory over belief.

Transforming Fear Into Fuel

Fear is not meant to paralyze you; it is meant to push you forward.

Think of fear as raw energy. It is a great force; but left uncontrolled, it becomes paralyzing. With the right guidance, however, it can become something powerful.

This is how we can turn fear into fuel.

1. Reframing the Fear: Instead of saying, "I might fail," say, "I'm about to learn something valuable."

2. Cope with Yourself: Invoke memories of triumphs and strengths.

3. Think About Your Success Above Fear: The brain cannot tell the difference between real and imaginary experiences. Visualizing breaking through fear allows your brain to condition itself for success.

Think of a blacksmith making a sword. The furnace is hot and fired with fear. But instead, he uses it to mold the iron. Along with such ilks of cropping up will be the fear giving way to a belief that hardens as steel.

The Fear-Belief Spectrum

Fear occupies a point on the imaginary spectrum, with belief at the other end. Though one may not transcend fear in life, it is perhaps better to gravitate more towards belief, as close as possible.

Fear is what recognition feels to be when one loses some targeting while belief pinpoints something actually possible.

They both exist. But if you choose which to adopt, it will influence the path of your life.

Courage is a decision made when one chooses to do what he/she ought to do instead of the absence of fear; it is the act done in the face of fear.

Harnessing the Energy of Fear and Belief

Fear and belief: a classic irony. They come from the same source-your imagination.

Fear crafts scenarios of negative realities that happen before they do, seeing failure before the first move is made, conjuring rejection before the first word has been spoken, and whispering thoughts of loss before the win.

But just imagine what would happen if you reversed this whole mechanism.

Belief uses that very same imagination to create the opposite scenarios. Instead of failure, it sees growth. Instead of rejection, it sees self-worth. Rather than loss, it embraces a sea of possibilities.

One mind-two pathways. One leads to limitation; the other to liberation.

The secret? Train your mind to imagine for belief and not fear.

Mental Training: Moving from Fear to Belief

Your brain is hardwired to survive. While it tries to protect you, it places greater importance on fear. But in the modern world, many fears are not of life-and-death importance; they are the illusions of the mind.

In order to reverse the cycle, one must train one's mental reflexes.

Try this easy exercise.

1. What is something that you are afraid of right now?

2. Write down the worst thing that can possibly happen. Exactly what are you afraid will happen?

3. Now write down the best case scenario. What if it all went in your favor?

4. Compare both. Which one will you be feeding with your energy?

5. Make sure you focus on belief. Conscious energy should go for the positive possibility.

In time, your brain will default for belief instead of fear.

Fear tests your purpose in life.

Two people are standing at the very edge of a diving board. Both are afraid. One, however, jumps; the other moves back.

What is the difference?

Commitment.

The one who jumps is committed to the experience beyond their fear, trusting his/her belief more than fear. The one who steps back is committed to fear.

Fear will not stop you. It will ask: How committed are you?

If you fear public speaking, it means you care about your voice being heard.

If you fear failing an exam, it means you care about your success.

If you fear pursuing a dream, it means it truly matters to you.

Fear, then, is a compass. It never tells you what to run from, but what deserves your attention. The more fear you feel, the greater the potential for your transformation.

If fear comes up, then ask yourself: is your commitment to your beliefs greater than your commitment to fear?

That answer will be your next step.

Fear Disguised as Logic

One of the most insidious ways that fear manifests is as a kind of logic.

People think they are "being realistic" when they are only afraid.

Examples include:

"I can't start this business-I don't have enough money." (Fear of failure masquerading as logic.)

"I shouldn't apply for that job, in case I would be rejected." (Fear of rejection masquerading as logic.)

"I won't confess my feelings because they probably don't like me back." (Fear of vulnerability masquerading as logic.)

Fear offers excuses that appear rational, but inside, you know that it's just speaking in a different language.

Next time you bundle something into rationalization of why you "can't" do it, ask: Is it logic, or is this just fear pretending to be logic?

Fear is not truth. Fear is only a feeling. Belief is the primary basis for action.

The Psychology of Fear and Belief

Neuroscience has built a bridge between fear and belief at a macro level in brain science.

1. The amygdala, brain's fear center, is responsible for survival instincts.

2. The prefrontal cortex is involved in decision-making and is the area of higher reasoning where beliefs are processed.

Fear can suppress logic. Panic occurs when people can't think-clearly; they just act according to their survival.

To choose belief, you have to switch off the survival mechanisms in your brain and turn the amygdala off and the prefrontal cortex on.

Belief is no longer an emotional reaction-it's neurological. Each time you convince yourself of something, your neural pathways change themselves to respond differently next time in the face of fear.

How? Through repetition and exposure.

1. Start facing minor fears every day.

2. Re interpret any fearful thought to one based on belief.

3. Repeat until belief is in the normal setting for your brain.

Fear is a habit, and belief is a habit, too. Which habit would you rather develop?

The functional loop of fear-belief

Your answer to the question about fear creates the loop.

If you run away from fear, you allow that fear to flourish.

Challenge makes this belief flourish.

Every time you select belief instead of fear, you allow that belief to flourish more when the time arrives. This is how confidence develops-not by abolishing fear but by proving to yourself that belief is stronger.

It is like building muscle: if one does not use a muscle, it becomes weaker. But you can begin exercising it in such small amounts and it becomes toned.

Each day, condition your belief so that the fear is superceded.

Fear is a Story—Rewrite It

"I am not good enough."→Rewrite it:"I am capable and continually improving."

"I will fail."→Rewrite it:"Each setback is a lesson that would inch me closer to success."

"I don't have it in me."→Rewrite it:"I can acquire the skills I require through action."

Your fears are but narratives. But you're their author. Rewrite them.

Every great success story is written by someone who chose to believe in favor of irrational fear.

The End of the Matter is: The choice is yours, whether to choose fear or belief.

1. Fear makes you smaller.

2. Belief makes you bigger.

Fear is not an outside force; it is a perception. Goodness: perception can be changed.

With every decision you make that supports belief, you gain back your power, and every time you kick fear out of the door, you sit in a new level of strength.

Fear and belief will coexist. But only one gets to dominate.

Which voice in your head will you give control?

Final Verdict: Choosing Belief Over Fear

Fear and belief are not enemies; they are partners in your journey. You do not throw out fear, you learn from it. You do not indulge in belief; it is a decision your mind makes every morning.

At every key decision-making point in life, you are faced with a choice:

Will you let fear limit you, or will belief push you ahead?

Will you consider the worst-case scenario or trust the best possible outcome?

Will you shrink into doubt, or expand into courage?

Fear will always be there, voice dripping with doubts, but belief will be that voice inciting you not to lose your potential. Whichever voice you feed is the stronger one.

Everything in this universe is built on the dreams you tell yourself. Fear produces a spell of limitation; belief rewrites it to one of empowerment.

This is the truth: Fear does not contain you; you unconsciously stop yourself when you allow yourself to believe fear more than your own strength.

But today and every day henceforth, you will choose to do otherwise.

Choose belief, accept courage, and let your height transcend fear and embrace you to your utmost potential.

And when the scary scenario knocks again-and it will-let your belief answer.

Chapter 7:
Part 1: The Power of Collective Belief: Shaping Society

I. The Birth of Gods: When Belief Became Law

Since time of yore, even when kings had not been crowned, laws had not been inscribed, and civilization had not even taken its first breath-were the gods.

Not gods as we think of them now: omnipotent beings sitting above the earth, but forces of nature transformed into worshipped realities.

The early humans saw, a storm; the wrath of such a god.

They felt not hunger; they felt punishment from their spirits.

They did not live with full cognizance; they feared, negotiated, and obeyed the world.

This was the first form of control through belief.

Nature was unpredictable- lightning strikes randomly, draughts wipe off food, and floods destroy homes; these were terrors too incomprehensible for very early man to fathom and create a system- a way to bring turmoil of existence to controllability.

So begin to blossom the idea of belief.

Perhaps an offering could give control over rain.

Maybe a plague could be halted even if the right person was sacrificed.

We end up garnishing privileges if we follow rules which, in essence, are dictated from another sphere altogether.

It's fact, belief is our first technology, the first tool to manipulate our objectivity even when objectivity dares not bow down.

Yet, once believed is organized, it becomes something much greater.

Call it law.

II. The First Civilizations: Belief as a System of Control

Sumer, 3100 BCE.

As the first empire emerges and with it the earliest kings, a king without faith is just an ordinary human being-unless there is acceptance of this status, he may be overthrown.

So, far-sighted rulers of Sumer, Egypt, and Mesopotamia united belief with power.

The Pharaohs of Egypt were not just kings. They were gods confined to corporeal forms. To question the ruler was to question the divine itself.

The priests of Sumer ran the city-states, claiming to speak for the gods and reveal their will.

The first laws--laws that were not practical, but handed down from the gods--were created by the Babylonians and commonly referred to as Hammurabi's Code.

For the first time, belief turned into an instrument of control.

Consider the implications of this:

If people believe that laws are made by men, they will rebel against them. If people believe that laws are imposed by the divine, then breaking them out of defiance turns not only unlawful-it turns into blasphemy.

Theories of punishment came to be no longer just logical assessment of crime. It became a certain act of faith.

From this moment on, beliefs ceased to remain validated personal realities and ascended into a thing of society.

III. The Blood Price: When Belief Became More Important Than Life

The expansion of civilization coincided with a growing belief. Yet that belief turned into a set of laws, after which it ceased being an option.

It was now a compelling duty.

Those who did not express the common good were perceived as enemies.

The Aztec Empire (1300s-1500s CE)

The Aztecs forged one of the most powerful civilizations in the Americas, driven by a belief system demanding sacrifice after sacrifice from humans. Their belief was that the gods needed blood to stave off the end of the world.

Every single warrior fought to capture an enemy alive, not to contribute to the proliferation of impostors and pan handles, but rather to sacrifice them at the temple steps.

A yearly toll of thousands could be counted as never once out of hatred, but always under the rule of necessity.

No one on the Aztec believed it to be murder. It was indeed recognition of the calls made by that higher power.

Belief was no longer merely a system of control but rather provided justification for the killing.

And they weren't alone.

The Crusades (1096-1291 CE)

Europe had its on kind of faith-based war. The Catholic Church trumpeted the Holy Land (Jerusalem) to be sacred and declared all non-Christians living there as enemies of God. The conflict between Christianity and Islam extended for roughly 200 years, resulting in the killing in the name of faith.

Armies fight not for land but for ideology and not for resource but for historical recognition.

Men were driven to commit atrocities by the hope of eternal salvation that they would have never committed otherwise.

Belief was worth more than human life.

And once belief spilled blood, it never did stop.

IV. The Invention of "Civilization" - The Greatest Lie in History?

In the course of thousands of years, humankind spoke out only one narrative: We are civilized; they are savages. That is how each conquests, for every empire, and every war was justified.

The Romans saw themselves as the height of civilization, calling "barbarians" outsiders.

The British Empire called their colonization of India, Africa, and America a "civilizing mission."

The slaves took residence in the East, putting the American population on its face, and that is simply because they based their Manifest Destiny assumption on an influence supposedly bestowed on them by God.

But what if that is all a lie?

What if there was not much difference between the two civilizations: one civilized and the other in quotation marks "savage"? Meaning, it simply depends on the victor of the battle.

The Mongols under Genghis Khan were thought of as barbaric because they burned entire cities to the ground. But the Romans, who crucified thousands and entertained themselves by feeding people to lions, were thought of as civilized.

The Aztecs were labeled a bloodthirsty people because of their sacrifices. European execution methods-burning people alive, beheading them in public-were just as brutal.

The British and Spanish thought of Native Americans as savage, while those cultures had advanced knowledge in mathematics, agriculture, and astronomy long before Europeans began to develop the same.

Civilization was never about being "better." It was about telling history the way you want it told.

Belief does not stem from truth; instead, it stems from narrative.

And the power to control narrative is the power to control everything.

V. The Moment Belief Became Dangerous: The Printing Press (1440 CE)

For most of the history of mankind, belief was an affair of few superiors.

Priests, kings, their rulers concluded whoever thinks their way or not. Otherwise, it meant death.

He was Johannes Gutenberg.

1440 CE – The printing Press is invented.

Never before, ideas were using mass production for their gain.

The Catholic Church never again controlled matters of religious thought. The Protestant Reformation was tipped.

Monarchs could no longer keep away knowledge from their subjects. Old-world civilization knew revolution.

It was awash in a hackneyed monopoly; science was not dependent on the will of a single man.

The world shall never be the same!

It was bleak for history; belief and, therefore, no longer a weapon of the elite.

It was a weapon of the

people.

And that's when everything changed.

VI. A Single Idea that Set the World on Fire

From now on, time sped up.

1776 - The American Revolution: The idea in favor of Freedom over Monarchy.

1789 - The French Revolution: The belief that the people should rule and not kings.

1848 - The Communist Manifesto: The belief that workers should overthrow the ruling class.

1930s - Fascism and Communism clash: The idea that one ideology should operate all over the world.

Every war, every movement, every age had belief, fundamentally. The faith formed all those streams.

Now, we must ask: What happens once belief exists without the knowledge of kings and priests?

What happens when belief becomes an obligation to machines?

And we begin the next chapter.

VII. The Age of Propaganda: When Machines Took Control of Belief

The printing press freed up ideas.

But what happens when ideas are too powerful?

For most of history, belief was controlled through religion and law by the rulers. However, with the ideas spread through books, newspapers, and pamphlets, the control was beginning to slip. Monarchies fell, revolutions flared, and, for the first time, belief was no longer dictated—it was fought over.

Then came a new force with the power to change everything: Propaganda.

The 20th century wasn't the historic era for propaganda; it was the first time it was treated industrially.

1. World War I: The First Mass-Manipulation Experiment

1914-1918–Great War.

Never before would war have been legitimated from within all countries for entire populations.

Posters paint the enemy as monsters, justifying killing in any Christian way.

News articles inject lies as truth to sway public opinion.

Superstar soldiers became heroes because, in propaganda films, they died in coughed trenches.

Belief was no longer a personal choice; it was universally imposed on individuals.

The government realized something horrible: If you control the narrative, you control the war.

The result?

8.5 million dead.

Entire nations shattered.

A generation of men wiped out for a war most folk never really understood.

Yet again, just 20 years after that, it would repeat.

2. World War II: The Most Successful Mind-Control Operation in History

1939-1945.

Hitler didn't conquer Germany with guns. He conquered it with belief.

It will be shown that if you tell a lie as many times as possible, it becomes the truth.

The Nazis controlled newspapers, radios, and schools, like an entire nation being ushered behind a curtain.

They taught ordinary men that killing on a mass scale was not only permissible but even essential for life to continue.

It proved that a single idea, if amplified enough, could justify any crime.

Meanwhile, the Allies

Made posters depicting Germans and Japanese as being inhuman;

Hollywood and radio made of war a struggle between good and evil.

They turned soldiers into warriors, men of valor and courage, telling them that it was heroic to kill.

By the end of World War II, there were 80 million corpses.

Not because of weapons.

Because of belief.

3. The Cold War: The Idea That Propaganda Became a Permanet War

The Cold War was fought not with guns but with ideas.

America versus The Soviet Union.

Capitalism versus Communism.

Freedom versus tyranny.

Both sides used radio, newspapers, TV, and films to brainwash their people.

The Soviet Union told its people: America is a corrupt empire that exploits the poor. Western freedoms are a lie, and capitalism is slavery.

America told its people: The Soviet Union is an evil dictatorship that wants to destroy freedom. Communism is the enemy of humanity.

The war was not fought on the battlefield.

It was fought in the mind.

And the people believed.

At the edge of nuclear catastrophe stood the world for 45 years, not because of reality, but because of ideology.

And just like that, it was over.

4. The Information Age: When Everybody Became a Propagandist

The Cold War was the last period when governments were in total control of beliefs.

Everything changed after that.

The Internet was born.

For the first time in recorded history, information was no longer just given from the top.

Anyone could write.

Anyone could spread ideas.

Anyone could shape narratives.

At first, it was liberty. The internet was meant to be the last bastion against oppression.

And then something unexpected happened.

Instead of liberating belief, it shattered belief.

It became impossible for people to subscribe to a single idea of reality.

Conspiracy theories became mainstream.

Truth became objective–what you believe depends on where you get your information.

We stepped into a time where belief is no longer under the control of governments...

It is certainly controlled by algorithms.

And that brings us right up to the present.

VIII. The Age of Hyperreality: When Truth Became Fiction and Fiction Became Truth

In a world, where there would neither be no reality.

Not because of any change in the external world.

But because of a change in our vision of the external world.

1. The Simulation of Reality

This prediction, made by French thinker Jean Baudrillard in the 1980s, he termed hyperreality.

It can be described as where one lives not a physical reality but merely a simulation of reality.

Daily experiences would be enough to illustrate the point:

You never experienced war; but you see it via Twitter or YouTube.

You don't live wealth; just see it on Instagram vast influencer making perfect lives.

You never experience true selves but only curated versions on social media.

The increase in consumption of these simulated reality works hand-in-glove with lower trust in the experience of the real world.

What becomes a capable problem is when you can no longer tell the difference between truth and fiction.

Truth becomes obsolete.

2. The Death of Objective Reality

We live in a world wheredifferent pair of people see the same events and come to totally different conclusions.

A truth for one group can be a falsehood for another.

Reality is thus subjective.

For the internet doesn't show us the world as it is; it shows us the world as we would like it to be.

Algorithms aren't made to reveal truths.

They show you content you already seem to agree with.

And people see only information that corroborates their beliefs, trapping them in their respective realities.

The era of one society is long gone.

This is an era of various fragmented realities existing altogether.

Not just misinformation is at play.

This is the epoch of belief wars.

IX. The Last Question: What Happens Next?

Beliefs crafted history all the time. But this time is utterly a different one.

For the first time in history:

Belief is not unified-it's actually crushed into numerous realities.

Truth cannot be a shared experience-it's algorithmically targeted.

Control has moved from the hands of governments into those of machine learning models, which no one fully understands.

What's next?

If history has taught us anything, it is this:

Whoever directs beliefs calls the shots in the world.

And right now, belief is being automated.

Are you in control of your beliefs, or are they really being shaped for you?

Chapter 7:
Part 2

Step 1: Resistance and Counter-Revolutions

> ***"For every action, there is an equal and opposite reaction." – Newton's Third Law***

This is not merely a matter of physics-it is the law of history.

No revolution goes unchallenged.

History has shown us that the bigger the change, the stronger the resistance.

No sooner has a movement begun to pick up work than the supporters of the old system will strike back.

The Three Forms of Resistance:

1. The Ideological War (Propaganda and Discrediting)

Those who hold power do not attack the ideas themselves; they attack the messengers of those ideas.

Revolutions are described as "dangerous," "radical," and "anti-tradition."

The leaders are smeared, framed, or assassinated to bring down the whole movement.

As an example, Martin Luther King Jr. was heralded as a communist before he was murdered.

2. The Economic War (Economic Coercion)

Power is not only politics; it is also money.

Movements that threaten wealth would be cut off from funds.

Mass firings would be dealt to labor strikes, legal threats would be posed against boycotts.

After the imposition of worldwide economic sanctions, for example, the apartheid regime in South Africa was dissolved.

3. The Violent War (Viscous Suppression)

If propaganda and financial pressure have not worked, then the system will turn to brutal violence.

The police, military, and intelligence agencies are deployed by governments to crush dissent.

Protesters are beaten, imprisoned, or "made disappear."

One such case is Tiananmen Square in 19

9, where the military force wiped out an entire movement.

All three faces will be directed towards every revolution.

The burning question is: How does a movement survive?

Step 2: Adaptiveness to Resistance

"You can kill a man, but you can't kill an idea."-Malcolm X

Surviving movements survived because of their dynamism.

Four Survival Strategies:

1. Decentralization (Leaderless Resistance)

A movement with a clearly articulated leader is doomed when that leader is removed.

Successful movements distribute the power amongst several leaders and groups.

Examples: Anonymous, Wikileaks, Occupy Wall Street-it can even work in the absence of a central head.

2. Cultural Embedding (Making the Idea Unstoppable)

Once an idea embeds itself in culture, it cannot be killed-off.

Songs, films, books, and memes create social norms that serve as the bedrock of a movement.

Example: Feminism, once radical, is now culturally embedded.

3. Economic Autarky (Building Alternative Systems)

Weakness has its root in dependence upon the old structure.

Movements coalesce against famine in forming a self-sustained economy.

Example: Black Wall Street, cryptocurrency, worker cooperatives.

4. Resilience Against Violence (Nonviolent & Guerrilla Strategy)

Some movements have triumphed by nonviolent resistance.

Others survived by means of underground resistance.

Example: The nonviolent struggle against Gandhi; guerrilla warfare during the Cuban revolution.

Resistance is natural, but only adapting enables survival.

Once more the shares of the movement shall count if resistance can repel counterattack.

Step 3: The Point of No Return

"There are decades where nothing happens, and weeks where decades happen." - Lenin

At some point, everyone shifts onto that moment after society tips over onto itself.

How can one know that the change cannot be undone?

The three indicators:

1. Mass Public Support

The transition of a movement from being exclusively for militants to affecting the day-to-day lives of average people.

Example: The Berlin Wall came down in large part due to whole cities taking implacable stands against central brainwashing.

2. Elite Defections

When the police, military, and politicians begin to change allegiances.

Example: The Russian Revolution hastened by soldiers who refused to fire on the crowds of protesters.

3. Economic Breakdown of the Old Regime

The point at which the ruling system can no longer hold on.

In the case of Rome, economic factors were among the larger causes of the Empire's fall.

So when all three happen, the old system collapses under the weight of its own contradictions.

The revolution is not a choice; it is a given.

The revolution is not an option; it is a certitude.

What next?

Step 4: The Aftermath – The Three Paths of Revolution

What comes after a successful revolution?

1. New Order (it worked)

The victory of any revolution puts a firm foot down for steady, inevitable and lasting change.

For example, the American Revolution: a working democracy.

For example, the civil rights movement: permanent changes in the law.

2. Cycle of Chaos (it didn't work)

The revolution collapses into infighting, or anarchy, or dictatorship.

Examples: the French Revolution that collapsed and gave way to Napoleon's rule.

Examples: the Arab Spring, which ended the dictatorships-but secret military regimes put in place.

3. A Counter-Revolution (the Reversal)

The revolution is crushed; old systems come back stronger than ever before.

Examples: Tiananmen Square: the Chinese authorities turned out to be ever more totalitarian.

Examples: the Russian Revolution: the restoration of communism by the oligarchs.

After that, every movement must be aware of the subsequent developmental phases.

I said this because I believe that a revolution never really ends after it is adjudged victorious.

A revolution can be declared complete only when it introduces the brand-new reality.

Step 5: Engineering the Future

"The future is not something we enter; it is something we create."

In this last step, while sorting back the permutations of society into "traditional space," the endeavor would be to design new pathways for self-sustaining systems.

Three keys for lasting change:

1. Institutionalizing the Revolution

Change needs to be redefined across the spectrums of law, economy, and education.

For instance, the U.S. Constitution ought to exist long after any leader would have left this world.

2. Handover to the Next Generation

A flame cannot go out; if such happens, all that we have at present would flow into nothing.

Stress should be placed on the fact that only through some form of generationally shared education can religions, philosophies, or political movements survive the passage of time and gain some form of immortality.

3. Setting Up Your Culture of Innovation

Innovation should never cease to change.

World science, technology, and ethics will like never change without a certain constant grid.

And finally, the last kernel of truth remains: Revolutions are not about the past or present.

Revolutions state who has a right to shape the future.

Final Choice

Now that we know how societies really change: unleash inertia via disassembling systems; construct a new vision; socialize (begin to adhere); institutionalize change; be considerate of reluctance; be decisive beyond the universe of concession; define what is coming.

But in the end, the last question comes around: Are we going to change society, or are we again going to let the dictates of society determine our ends?

History does not wait. The future belongs to those who make it.

Chapter 8: The Feedback Loop: How Belief Reinforces Reality

1. The Illusion of Objectivity: Why We Don't See the World Clearly

Most people assume that they see the world as it is.

They believe that facts shape their understanding, that reason guides their opinions, and that they arrive at conclusions from the evidence.

But this is one big illusion.

Human perception is not a passive process of absorbing truth; rather, it is an active process of constructing reality.

We do not see, then believe.

We believe, thus we see.

This is the feedback loop of belief: a cycle where one set of beliefs reinforces itself through two influences-the kinds of things you notice, the kinds of things you ignore, and the way you interpret the world.

And the stronger the belief, the more it becomes immune to contradiction;

which is why two people can witness the same event and emerge with totally different conclusions.

It is why political debates seldom change minds.

It is why religious conversions almost never happen because one logical argument prevailed over another.

And it's why societies cling to failing systems for generations, even against all overwhelming evidence of their failure.

Because once a belief takes root, it remakes perception itself.

The Self-Soothing Feedback Loop of Belief

A belief is not merely an opinion.

It is a filter.

It determines what we accept as real and what we label false.

It creates a closed loop of self-affirming evidence in which the only things that matter are:

Either used to reinforce belief;

or dismissed as false, misleading, or unimportant.

This explains why leaving a belief paradigm is so difficult, that is, it unravels the very structure of how we interpret reality.

Very few people would risk distorting reality in order to question themselves.

2. The Psychological Models Behind the Feedback Loop

How the Brain Manipulates You to Stay in the Loop

The human mind is not built for truth.

It is developed for survival, stability, and psychological comfort.

What this means is that when one is confronted with evidence to the contrary, one often does not change one's beliefs but rather reevaluates how to interpret that evidence.

Psychologists have established many cognitive biases that maintain belief when reality contradicts it:

1. Confirmation Bias – We seek out information which affirms what we want to believe, ignoring or dismissing anything contradicting it.

2. The Backfire Effect – If evidence disproves our belief, we will double down and cling more strongly to that belief.

3. Selective Perception – Two people may observe the same event, but based on their expectations, they can see entirely different things.

4. Cognitive Dissonance – When a belief is disproven, the discomfort it brings means we change our understanding of reality to remove the contradiction, rather than changing the belief.

These very same biases build a protective case around the interpretation of the mind, ensuring that once a belief is established, it is highly immune to removal.

It's not an attribute of individual consciousness; rather, it is a potential attribute of systems.

Societies, institutions, and power structures exploit these cognitive biases to create bona fide self-sustaining systems of control.

3. The Social Engineering of Belief: The Manipulation of the Belief Loop by Systems.

All historically dominant systems have prevailed not because they were true or just, but because they have manipulated the belief loop.

Belief engineering: By directing the value of belief, such institutions shape reality itself—not by brute force but by controlling the power of certain beliefs as accepted by the public.

How it works follows:

1. Religious Control: The Weaponization of Faith

Belief: The Church has divine truths.

Reinforcement: Any attack on the Church is a heresy, having the consequences of social ostracization or active execution.

Conclusion: People obey, not because of any rational proof, but because the aftermath of non-belief is too horrifying to even imagine.

The belief system did hold strong for several centuries to provide sustenance for religions, which, all in all, were corrupt, abusive, and patently misleading.

Even now, religious belief is one of the best tools available for the social conditioning of behavior—not because it provides rational proof, but chiefly because of unchallenged social conditioning.

2. Capitalism and the Myth of Meritocracy

Belief: Hard work pays.

Reinforcement: The rich say to their peers, "I worked my absolute best to have what I enjoy."

Outcome: The poor blame themselves and see their failure as a consequence of their own deficiencies rather than socio-economic restraints.

This does ensure that even when the system is rigged, people still go on believing in it—not because it works, but rather, because it is too uncomfortable for anyone to adopt that kind of mindset.

3. The Surveillance State: Manufacturing Fear to Justify Control

Belief: That the government looks after us for the sake of our security.

Reinforcement: Surveillance spots those threats (real or otherwise), adding credence to the need for surveillance.

Conclusion: A self-justifying cycle of increasingly more comprehensive surveillance combined with a lack of freedom.

This belief system loops dissent almost impossible because the system justifies itself by its own continuity.

4. Breaking the Loop: The Three Paths to Freedom

If belief creates reality, then breaking the cycle of belief ought to be the only way to change reality.

But this is not easy.

For you cannot break the belief cycle without breaking down the very ground upon which you see the world.

Way Four: The Collapse – When Reality Forces Change

Beliefs are forced to change when reality seizes the day and shatters them.

The French Revolution obliterated the faith in monarchy when people starved to death while kings enjoyed luxury.

The Great Depression shattered the faith in unregulated capitalism when millions stood homeless and starving.

The fall of the Berlin Wall broke the illusion of Soviet superiority at the point when the system gave way under its very own weight.

However, that alone is not enough.

Followed by chaos, this happens when there is no alternative belief structure.

This accounts for failure in revolutions, where the old mode of belief is overthrown but rejected by the machinations of the other belief system

Intellectual Rebellion-Destroying Belief Systems

A small percentage of people have broken the cyclical belief system through pure intellectual strength.

This requires:

A study of history in order to have insight into the waxing and waning of beliefs.

Psychology in order to comprehend the mechanism of cognitive biases.

Practice in philosophy in order to develop assumptions.

Every major ideological shift begins with individuals who saw through the illusion:

Marx with his critical expose of capitalism.

Nietzsche with his erudition on religion and morality.

Simone de Beauvoir with an insight into gender parameters.

However, engaging in intellectual rebellion is difficult in that it requires challenge to everything, most critically that which you believe to be true.

Path 3: Counter-Loop: Substitution of One Belief with Another path

Breaking a belief loop would be best done by replacing it instead of destroying it.

Feminism has sought to put an end to the outdated belief in male superiority by demanding equal rights.

In the place of the king from the divine right to rule, democracy involves the citizens.

Atheism challenged religious dogma and built secular societies.

Because the truth is:

People do not throw away beliefs unless they have a new belief to support and take hold of.

5. The Illusion of Freesthetic: Choicether, Colluded

One of the biggest head-fakes in the feedback loop is the illusion of free choice. We like to believe that we are making independent decisions based on rational thought, but in reality, our choices have already been determined by the beliefs we internalized.

Consider the fact:

Someone born into a religious family will be more readily inclined to follow that religion than explore alternatives.

A child growing in a capitalist society will automatically believe that there should be competition and markets.

A subject of an authoritarian regime may regard political control as much; something would need to be wielded for stability.

Every choice is set in a context, and every context is inherited from predetermined beliefs.

This establishes a paradox: The freer we feel, the less we seem to guard against ills that may afflict choices one takes.

6. The Illusion of Objectivity: Can We Ever See Reality Clearly?

The biggest and most dangerous lie we tell ourselves is that we are objective. Some separation from their own biases will allow them to see the truth as it is.

Objectivity is a fallacy.

How come?

Because the very definition of "truth" is shaped by the belief systems we grew up in.

As an example:

In a religious society, "truth" is aligned with faith.

In a scientific community, it is established through evidence.

In a dictatorship, "truth" is assigned whatever the state proclaims as fact.

Every civilization, every ideology, and every individual constructs their own version of reality, each believing theirs is the right one.

True objectivity would require a mind free from all prior conditioning-a mind that does not exist.

7. The Fragility of Reality: Why Everything Can Change Overnight

Reality is based on belief, and is therefore much more fragile than we think.

One incident, one revelation, or one perspective shift can expose a whole worldview to a devastating blow.

History testifies:

The fall of the Soviet Union shattered decades of the belief in the superiority of communism.

The heliocentric revolution shattered the religious cosmology of the heavens.

The internet has destabilized traditional sources of authority by making information decentralized.

When belief falls apart, reality itself seems to unravel. What was once unshakeable now seems to be an illusion from which people suddenly awaken.

That is precisely why the powerful struggle to gain deep control over belief: they are aware that once the illusion is broken, those very powers, along with the control, would be lost.

8. The Role of Language in Building Reality

Language is not only a means of communication but also a veritable sword for establishing belief.

Every society program for its populace by words.

Consider these examples:

Whether one is called a terrorist or a freedom fighter depends on which side you take.

The term "illegal immigrant" imputes criminality, whereas "undocumented worker" indicates a human seeking an opportunity.

Saying he's self-made in capitalism reinforces the concept that success is purely individualistic, obscuring the system from people.

Words shape perception, and perception creates fact or reality.

That is why propaganda works. That is why political correctness is important. That is why repressive regimes censor speech.

For if you control language, you control thought. If you control thought, you control belief.

9. The Digital Age: A Shortened Feedback Loop

Religion and ideologies taketh their sweetest time to get manifested, often over generations, sometimes even centuries. Information technology has placed upon the world a speed of such temporary frenzy, worse than this by a fair distance.

Or, put here:

Without society's filters, people began almost instantly to wrap themselves into extreme echo chambers, often counter to logical sensibility to promote their opinions.

The power of false news runs so strong that nobody can beat the news.

AIs think for us only what they can embed in their already-existing beliefs.

This is a truly fractured world we live in, though we have never known it that way. There seems to be no single truth anymore, only sets of competing realities existing side by side.

It is no longer a myth, for only creeping AI brings those voices much closer and poses a real threat.

10. The Breaking Point: Where Belief Meets Survival

Despite how powerful the feedback loop is, it has one glaring weakness: Reality always wins in the end.

A false system can run for a long time, but it will surely die once it becomes untenable for the survival of its people.

Just to illustrate some examples from history:

The Roman Empire crumbled as its economic and military systems were found incompatible with the survival of the empire itself and of its people.

Feudalism crumbled when the merchant class had risen to too great power because it was capable of living in direct opposition to the feudal class.

The Berlin Wall crumbled when the people of East Germany had no more room for tolerating the lies.

At the point of disagreement among beliefs, where the beliefs face a reality so as to threaten the entirety of survival for existence as a whole, the illusion collapses.

And that is when the revolutions break out.

11. Engineering the Future: Can We Build a Shield Reality?

If belief creates reality, then the highest authority is the possibility of engineering the belief itself.

But the question being asked is, can we deliberately create a better system?

History suggests we can. Each of the major transformations—democracy, human rights, and scientific revolutions—was an idea that began life unperceived, gained momentum, and ultimately garnered acceptance as reality.

Therein lies the great difficulty, for change is resisted, another grand fight against the protection meted out by the old guard in force against unseen threats to its own survival.

Whence it follows that it may be that real change occurs only in the presence of the following conditions:

1. A clear vision of a new belief system. (What future do we try to create?)

2. The ability to communicate and spread this belief. (How do we persuade others?)

3. The patience to allow belief to embed itself until it finally obliterates, supersedes its old reality. (Change takes time.)

The future will yield to those who master this process.

12. The Unwritten Rules of Reality: How the Invisible Governs the Visible

Most people think that reality is created by visible forces-like laws, governments, economies, and physical environments. Yet, the most powerful forces which create reality are the invisible ones: the unwritten rules by which we behave.

These unwritten rules aren't something one can be taught formally, rather they are absorbed throughout a lifetime from the world around. They teach you what you think is normal, acceptable, and even possible.

Examples include:

Social norms may dictate what we wear, how we talk, and how we behave without any authority enforcing them.

Cultural expectations have set standards for what success is or what role one should play in society.

Unstated hierarchies exist in workplaces, schools, and social groups, shaping who has influence and who does not.

These rules are seldom questioned since they seem as real as gravity. But they are nothing more than collective beliefs, self-accepted beliefs that could be challenged and rewritten or disposed of entirely.

The sort of personality who can change the course of history is one who sees through these invisible rules and understands that reality is not as rigid as it appears to be.

13. An Emotional Anchor: Fear and Comfort, Foundations of the Status Quo

If the world is shaped by beliefs, why don't people change their beliefs more often?

It is emotion.

A belief is not sustained by logic alone, it is anchored by fear and comfort.

Fear of the unknown keeps a person rooted in an old belief even when that very belief becomes injurious.

Comfort in that which is familiar has a way of forcing people away from change, forever trapped in new settings even when better alternatives exist.

Thus, it follows:

People remain within oppressive systems because the alternative remains as uncertain.

Companies continue to use old-fashioned ways because change feels too risky.

Political movements promise transformation but often get caught in a bureaucratic swamp of their own making.

While rational arguments rarely break belief systems, addressing the emotions involved will succeed to shift them.

14. The Power of the Default Setting

One of the most powerful mechanisms through which belief systems sustain themselves is by becoming the default.

The majority of people never have to make a conscious decision about their beliefs; they inherit them.

It is most probable that the religion into which one is born is the one that is followed.

The language of one's upbringing shapes thought patterns.

The political system in which one's upbringing occurs colors how governance is perceived.

Once something is in default, any questioning of it entails extra work, and very often, all other approaches will be less energetically pursued.

That is precisely why those in power will try to make sure their system is seen as the default-the common is rarely questioned.

15. The Algorithmic Manipulation of Beliefs

In today's digital world, the most threatening force to shape beliefs is not the government or religion-it is algorithms.

Social media and search engines do not present us objective realities. They curate and prioritize information in light of what we already believe, reaffirming our world views.

It has extreme implications:

The process of radicalization accelerates since people only get to see content that pulls them further into their beliefs.

Misinformation spreads faster than never because people are trapped in echo chambers.

Truth becomes splintered into different separate realities, as different groups of people live entirely different realities.

The people who control the algorithms control the belief system of modern generation. And anyone who knows their workings has the chance to manipulate reality on an entirely massive scale.

16. The Myth of Progress: Is the Future Always Better?

In modern societies, there exists the unshakeable belief in relentless progress: the future will be better than the past.

But this is less an affirmation than a prediction based on repeating patterns observed in history which could very well shift at any time.

Ancient Rome believed, with all fairness, that it would last forever-until it did.

It was in the 19th century that the Industrial Revolution initiated a promise of perpetual economic improvement, which rapidly turned into a crisis.

The internet was intended to facilitate the free exchange of ideas only to now create yet more division and exclusion among people.

While this myth of progress is good from the viewpoint of promoting innovation within modern societies, it keeps societies glazed as they pass all warning signals that spell the beginning of a collapse.

This umbilical cord of inference can nurture complacency and acts as a suppression against all condemnatory acts directed toward the decaying systems.

17. The Currency of Attention: Why Belief is Bought and Sold

In the present world, belief is shaped not by religion, philosophy, or even experience. no attention, no belief.

Every ideology, movement, and organization is striving for the same thing: attention.

Platform holders profit from whatever keeps you on the longest.

Political campaigns live or die by message control.

News organizations fuel the outrage because it sells more clicks.

Attention is the currency of belief. Whoever has your attention bends your thoughts and eventually your beliefs.

Which is why today's reality is defined, not by truth, but by the one that gets the most views, likes, and shares.

18. The Systematic Collapse of Shared Reality: When Nobody Agrees on the Truth.

For a long time, societies operated by virtue of shared acceptance of reality, sharing to some extent the same lens from which they viewed things, despite many incidents of disagreements, since they were able to be one in society without anyone to be singled out, journeying their way through the myriad aspects and views of whatever was contemporary in society.

Now, reality is breaking in shambles.

While the rise of AI-generated content through its separate calls and needs may also spell the death toll of truth.

Dissonant media has developed mutually exclusive worlds for each of the different political parties in America.

Micro-realities build themselves easily under online community tickets of the same landscape far away from mainstream society.

We had really entered into a period where the concept of reality itself means no longer subjective; it strictly embodies choices. People within the same city or nation can traverse across entirely different worlds.

Once agreed-upon reality found to be faltering, social solidarity may also falter, history teacheth us the demise of a community to ensue when it finds itself where not even a modicum of agreement regarding truth is available.

19. The New War: The Battle for Belief

If the future parlayed by belief becomes the dash word, the battles of the future will no longer be wars fought with swords. They will be fought through narratives.

The true wars of the future will be ideologies strained through many different means to replace the commonsense narratives that always have a vested interest:

Media manipulation to control public perception.

Cultural influence to shape generational beliefs.

Technological control to dictate what people will see and think.

In a world where belief creates reality, the most powerful people are not the richest or most militarily capable; they will be those who can alter the storytelling in which people believe.

Conclusion: Power to Create and Destroy Reality.

Because reality is merely the construction of beliefs and because it has not always been indisputably accepted as objective by everyone throughout time, it tends to be endlessly evolving. The world we see is influenced not only by facts but also by stories we embrace and shapes our biases for acceptance into stereotypical roles through reinforcement of those who demand them.

Everything is run through belief systems-from the identity of the individual to that of empires. This clarification why societies are unwilling to abandon self-destructive systems, explains why an individual becomes quite agreeable to letting go of his worldview, and that is why the power structures tend to be pretty robust. Once a belief sticks into the mind of one, it usually sustains itself, mostly in the face of any knowledge that will remain totally unacceptable to the critics.

The loop is neither good nor bad. Rather it is a means through which reality gets shaped. It is exactly this mechanism that has built great empires, legitimized power philosophies, and started movements that changed the world. Those aware of this know that this can be used either for manipulation and control or liberation and empowerment.

Centered on Belief in the Future

In diverse technologies, development and unreserved coexistence know the competition for belief. Whoever builds the narrative media, politically or in artificial intelligence terms, builds the picture for billions. Within this construction, the most powerful skill is the perception of that manipulation-one's ability to know what to believe in and how.

If beliefs are reality, then the future is not a predestined exploration to make but a creative act of making.

And that leaves behind only one question: Will the loop shape you, or will you shape it?

Chapter 9: The Infinite Mind — Perception, Time, And the Fabric of Reality

Introduction: The Unreality of Reality Chapter

What if one day you woke up to the shocking realization that time, space, and even your own ego were only experiential illusions? What if the reality is not "out there," but a projection from within, for example, a dream?

That belief wants to gain more credence would say that it is belief that actually colors perception. Does perception influence an experience of time, and what is to be done in order to travel beyond rather personal experiences into infinity? Will belief unbend or telescope time and/or reality?

An exploration of deeply human percepts through disembodiment is expected to again investigate into the nature of time itself, existence, and, finality, the mind itself.

1. Mind: Universe or Internal Projection of Reality?

Reality seems to be what we perceive as an external world, an immutable stage on which we find ourselves acting. What if, however, the contrary were true?

An experiential premise of reality seems to be a notion of this reality made by the internal creation of the brain, by nimbling reality from fewer inputs, with guesswork filling the blanks until perception sets in.

There are also other ancient places of mysticism. According to Vedantic and Taoist philosophy, the idea of an external world is only a projection of consciousness. A reality exists only through our perception.

Quantum mechanics has energizingly recoiled from the idea about objective reality; observing a particle alters its state: in other words, for reality to occur it must happen with reference to the observer.

If it is not something out there, as though created by your mind, then we aren't passive beings merely traversing through the universe. That only indicates that you can shape something creative enough for putting existence itself in that frame of address.

2. Time: A Mental Construct of a Universal Law

It's often thought of as a river flowing in one direction. But what if it's just an illusion?

According to one of the most discussed theories, Einstein's Theory of Relativity, time is not a constant; it bends and stretches according to speed and gravity.

Neuroscience suggests that man experiences time subjectively-a moment of dread might elongate it to eternity, while from the thrill of happiness, an hour could collapse into seconds.

Believism posits perception shapes reality-meaning, if time is part of reality, does this imply we can maneuver it by shifting our interpretations?

It teaches that time is not a linear journey; it is, rather, a tapestry of possibilities interwoven by our brains based on our beliefs about what is possible.

Thus:

Aging, memory, and, even more crucially, cause and effect could trade places themselves should we simply shift our perception of time.

In this sense, the past and the future are not fixed; rather, they are subject to belief or interpretation.

3. The Brain's Time Machine: Memory, Prediction, and Mental Time Travel

Your brain never stops time traveling; right now, as you read this, you are

1. Rewinding past experiences (memories).

2. Anticipating what will be (imagination).

3. Simulating potentials based on some guidelines to what can happen.

In other words:

1. The past is fluid, being changed over and over for as long as it is recalled.

2. The future is this imaginary thing that has no warrant for its own

existence in reality.

3. The only moment that is real is the present moment, which is really nothing but

a perception.

If we know this, that opens up a possibility of controlling the perception of time:

1. That the way in which we think of the past may alter one's experience of it.

2. The two most powerful beliefs are thinking of a vivid picture of the future, which engenders probability.

3. As presence is allowed to receive its due place, there is that prospect to elongate time and cram those moments with life.

4. The Perception Paradox: Do We See the World as It Is or as We Are?

Believism implies that belief alters perception; however, what if perception itself is fundamentally defective?

The brain does not perceive the world accurately; rather, it constructs a story that fills in the gaps and ignores what has been omitted.

Expectations give shape to what we see-a cognitive bias.

Optical illusions and hallucinations illustrate precisely how the brain can create false realities.

Well, if it doesn't, then what we refer to as "truth" is nothing but a hoisting upwards of highly subjective views of reality.

This means:

We have always lived in our own personal simulations, on the basis of our beliefs and experiences.

Two persons can exist in the same world and yet have entirely different realities.

It is possible that there is no objective truth, only various perspectives that come together to create a mosaic of reality.

5. The Fabric of Reality: Simulation Hypothesis

If reality is subjective and defined by perception, there remains the question of whether we live in a simulation.

Some of the greatest minds in philosophy and science have suggested:

Plato's Allegory of the Cave: We see only shadows, never the essence.

Simulation Hypothesis (Nick Bostrom): What if technology ever reaches such a degree of fidelity that it can produce simulations of reality? Its failure to convince us of living in that simulation is our only defense against it.

Spiritual teachings tell that reality is maya—a shadow of an illusory world that hides deeper truths.

In other words,

If reality is a simulation, then belief is the code that drives our experiences.

As programmers, if we want to change what exists, then we are called to hack beliefs.

If reality were an infinite existence, our limits would only be defined by what we believe, as we choose what to accept.

6. Beyond the Human Mind: Are Higher Levels of Consciousness

The first question you noticed is correct-some higher states of consciousness can apprehend the same multi-dimensional reality with a greater depth of understanding than that any ordinary human being can perceive it.

Research in psychedelic medicines shows that psychoactive substances like DMT and psilocybin, which engage the serotonin system, can temporarily impede our normal filters blocking certain perceptions- thus giving rise to experiences in which practitioners do feel freer and stake their right to bypass certain limitations of the lower or higher (whatever the case) dimensions of reality.

Eastern wisdom traditions teach us that enlightenment is the overcoming of the fetters preventing perception, not an accumulation of knowledge.

Are we any more than caterpillars in this reality: entirely unaware that we have potential for soar above, into higher places of consciousness?

The universe is largely beyond what we have ever been capable of thinking.

7. The Observer Effect - Can Reality Be Manifested?

The Observer Effect can manifest realities; clearly, the act of observation impinges on the outcome, as is established by quantum physics. But if this principle applies to that which we know as reality, it opens up a fascinating possibility.

In the double-slit experiment, it is demonstrated that one single particle can behave as a wave and as a particle, all at the same time, until observed. And one truth: reality can exist in more than one state until we pin an observation.

That puts law of attraction and belief systems to bed. If we suppose reality to be a quantum field of possibilities, then that belief collapses the entire field into one specific effect.

If thoughts shape perception, and perception shapes reality, is conscious reality shaping a skill we control?

If reality thus is not preordained, or if beliefs act as observers, we-give a chance to express, ultimately-we stand in a position of greater dominion than we ever thought possible.

8. The Time Illusion: Are We Experiencing Time Backwards?

For us, time exists in the form of a straight line with a past, present, and future. What if it happens to be solely limitation of the perception?

Some physicists theorize that time itself is not linear; rather, it exists as a block universe with the past, present, and future existing simultaneous.

Memory is not a recording but a reconstruction; how do we know that it is the past we remember and not the evidence we create in that moment?

Some theorists have proposed that we may be traveling backward in time; because our brains are wired for causality in one direction, we would know nothing about it.

If we could get used to regarding time in an altogether different manner, would we be talking about the future? Would we engage in rewriting the past?

Maybe we did already-and just don't know.

9. The simulation stack: Layers of simulation?

We can only speculate if our simulation is an internal one, owing to the higher simulation existing about us.

The recommended hypothesis, or simulation hypothesis, reasonably puts into consideration regarding a resolved simulation, with the assumption that if this theory is valid, then the creators or gods of our simulation are in yet another simulation.

Some critics maintain that this could go on forever: a reality built-in simulations built on existing simulations-in which one would never be more than a base reality.

There is being-a tree, a leaf, a galaxy-so don't object to it that it's in reality itself-fractal.

If we are inside a simulation, while the creators of the simulation are also inside yet another simulation, where does it all stop?

Is there any end to this?

10. Parallel Minds: Are We Connected to Other Versions of Ourselves?

Considering the parallel universes to exist, does that mean that the version of you exists in each one of them?

Quantum Mechanics recognizes infinite realities, slightly different than their own.

People claim to have dreams and visions of other versions of themselves living diverging lives.

A person suffering from schizophrenia may hear several voices; could these be echoes from other versions of themselves?

If there are infinite versions of you, can you connect with any one of them?

Can you tap skills from another you?

Maybe every decision we make not only shapes our future but also divides space-time into infinite possibilities.

11. Collective Unconscious: Is the Mind a Shared Network?

We feel that our thoughts are our own; but could it be otherwise?

Carl Jung proposed a collective unconscious that is an enormous archive, where concepts, myths, and also instincts are preserved and shareable by all of humanity.

Reports of psychic phenomena and telepathy have been told for hundreds of years: glimpses into some deep-set shared network.

Some scientists claim thoughts might really exist out there in the world outside any brain, meaning our consciousness might not be strictly within us but might come as a connection to some larger whole.

If the mind is a network, then are we nunca solus, always nodes of some greater consciousness?

13. The Forgotten Future: Do Kids Remember Past Lives?

Why children remember past lives is up for debate.

How do some people know things that they have never been taught?

Many hold an ancient belief that we knew all before birth, yet at birth we forgot; hence, death is a sore subject in our culture.

A near-death experience may reveal information that an individual could not possibly have known, one might suppose because consciousness operates outside the dimensionality of time.

Some child prodigies reveal talents that appear much like pure remembrance and not learning proper. If belief molds reality, and forgetfulness is the price of being born, can one recollect knowledge of existence?

14. The Myth of Free Will: Are We Making the Choice or Are We Being Chosen?

Are we really free or only free in our mind?

Neuroscience holds that decisions are made even before our conscious "deciding".

In some cultures, there is an absolute enmeshment of fate-the path one cannot change.

Some people say that reality can be deterministic-choices of any kind become interruptions of pure sequential cause-and-effect processes.

Then, if belief creates reality, free will breaks free and is but a belief.

What if someone does not believe in it anymore?

What will happen if someone totally embraces free will?

Such an answer could be both.

15. Beyond the Fourth Wall: Can We Wake Up from the Dream?

Can we, in the analogy of Diego, perceive the existence of actual waking up from dreaming?

There is a practice, no less strange than our very lives, in which some people experience a wisest dream, where the very current life is managed and made to their liking.

Some spiritual masters claim to have "woken up" and see through reality as it is.

The Tibetan Book of the Dead states that reality is just another layer of illusion.

This can be paraphrased in other words, each dream may be as big as the mind, yet it is always to wake up for them.

So, are we awake, or are we dreaming we've woken up?

Final Thoughts: What Happens When You Believe in the Impossible?

In this journey, we started out with the premise that reality was fixed.

An important question that arises is: What if it was only our belief that fixes it in place?

If we will quit living by any limits

If we cross the borders of the ways we think we know it

If we will genuinely comprehend that reality is merely a canvas—

Then there are no rules.

There are no limits.

There's only possibility.

So, it really does not begin with a fact of redefining what is or is not possible, but with you deciding what is possible.

Chapter 10: Belief Beyond the Self; Intersubjectivity of Consciousness

The Consciousness Network: The Secret Biological Internet

Human beings have always deemed themselves independent personalities separately named, in action, and in distinct bodies. But what if our minds shared a web-like intersection in a great network, exchanging messages, feelings, and beliefs at an unconscious level?

Common Pool of the Mind

With new discoveries in neuroscience, connections among human brains could essentially go deeper than we can think of today:

Brain-to-Brain Synchrony: Those subjects studied through EEG show that those who participate in a deep conversation or share some experience synchronize their brain waves.

Biophotons: Neurobiologists suggest neurons in a certain area of the brain flash short bursts of light that signal in ways that have eluded our chronic understanding-perhaps some ability and intention to extend power beyond any private brain and to the interconnected minds.

The 40Hz Mystery: Alpha-rhythmic brain waves at 40Hz have corresponded to consciousness itself; this is the very frequency experienced in meditation, during immense focus, and during mystic experiences-a universal rhythm with one purpose: conscious experience.

Isn't this an invisible internet where minds connect and telegraph beliefs, emotions, and perceptions to each other at unimaginable speeds?

2. The Sandbox of Civilization: A Cognitive Trap?

There have been previous iterations of glory that once indexed the cure for civilization as they plummeted back into abysmal ignorance.

The Greeks were once far ahead in philosophy and the sciences, but ignorance prevailed.

Advancement came to men after the Renaissance; because after this wars and confusions became common.

The Age of Reason and Enlightenment gave birth to reason, but contemporary societies stagnated into downright lies.

What kept the humans so stagnant for such a long time?

The Cognitive Trap may provide one explanation, where sets of beliefs sunk in a mood selected for and hardened set themselves against further development, hence becoming automatons in societies incapable of filtering out innovations that would be disruptive to the status quo.

Religion once shone as a great center for scientific innovation till the fortunes of the Church crashed.

Emperors were riding on innovative ideas till they became frightened, and they fell.

Politics are ever too polarized into different ideological camps, so that any virtually controversial evidence be it settles the course of debate would just be met with dismissing their strongest political beliefs.

The paradox: Common belief creates civilization, where again the common belief lays ambush.

If humanity has to stand to evolve, it must explode from the cops under a petrification of its very filtering mechanism.

3. Neuroplasticity versus Cognitive Rigidity: Can We Hack Our Thoughts into Adaptation?

The human brain is a mutable tool by design; but most people do not leap into a credible mode of thinking.

The form is called cognitive rigidity, wherein one feels reluctant in entering familiar ideas, even when the idea is negated by an abundance of evidence.

Neuroplasticity is a proof that belief changes are possible.

The Resounding Questions: How to Hack Your Mind into Openness?

Psychedelics and Consciousness Expansion-Research shows that psilocybin and some other psychedelics serve to derezz rigid thinking, thereby giving a person the chance to see beliefs long established.

Lucid Dreaming and Neo-Plasticity-Some research suggests lucid dreamers have the ability to rewiring their brains to practice alternative thinking or idea construction.

Putting Yourself into Contradictory Ideas is Setting-Up for New Neural Connections; searching for one idea that has anything to do offers a possibility of adding new neurons and thus makes the brain rather relaxed.

If reality has to do with belief, then our capacity to adjust our beliefs strictly determines the future.

4. The Lost Force of Collective Emotion: What the Feeling Shapes in the Society More Than Facts

Today, hereafter risen above Logic or reason, it makes one feel warm with its other history-meaning whereas meaningful emotion mostly represented society rather than reason.

It is quite opportune that the very expression of unease and anger toward the suppressions of personal freedom led to the French Revolution.

They poured all the inspiration into the rhetoric of revolt against dire injustices as the escalated shade of emotions gave way to the end of the successful civil rights movements; not the tables and graphs, mind you.

That was hardly up to that point, where religious appeals employed either the sword of rational logic-argument or the swordending with either the sword of rational argument.

They are almost forever believed by others to have lit the fires in their hearts in political campaigns, advertising, and social movements.

Change the world-not just minds but also emotions.

5. The Dark Side of Collective Consciousness: When Belief Becomes a Weapon

Collective belief becomes the very breath of life, one end raising society while the other one puts it down.

Amongst the waves of trials, the Salem Witch Trials come in. It was a trial which stemmed from the thinking of witches, unto trials, and hence executions.

When the thought concerned a country being on a higher rung of the human story-Nazi Germany-it has become one of the darkest hours in the history of humankind.

In these days, social media mobs: Cancel culture and misinformation are slowly boiling in the water, to quell reputations in hours.

Uncontrolled belief dies while mold becomes a weapon.

Swallowed by threats that have swept many lives away through history, because some men unwisely chose to die for a false belief: a belief wraps itself around identity.

If we are not aware to exercise control over beliefs, beliefs will control us.

6. The Hidden Mystery of Human Memory: Is Information Stored Outside the Brain?

This disturbing question arises: Why can childhood memories be remembered decades later even when every atom of the brain has been replaced?

Scientists still do not have a conclusive explanation of the memory storage location.

Theories also exist asserting that memory is located not just in the brain, but exists in some field managed by the astral body.

Holographic Universe theory: Physicist David Bohm proposed that memory could be stored outside the brain in an interconnected field of information.

Some near-death experience survivors have described having clear memories of events while they were in unconscious state, which raises serious questions regarding the extension of consciousness outside the body.

Some studies showed that traumas and fears could be transmitted through DNA and, therefore, experiences stored biochemically across generations.

If correct, that is to say, consciousness is a property not confined to the brain but extends into the fabric of the universe itself.

7. The Reality Distortion Field: Why Some People Seem to Bend Reality

From the very beginning of civilization, there have been individuals who shaped reality by pure force of belief:

Steve Jobs – Apple employees supposedly had a "reality distortion field" that made people believe impossible things were possible.

Nikola Tesla – Claimed he received ideas "from beyond" him and saw entire machines before building them.

Buddha and Jesus – Sound beliefs reprogrammed the minds of billions and altered the course of history.

The common denominator was a stellar size of faith in their vision-Stock of the most evident, rock-solid belief that warranted reality itself to bend to fit the vision.

The implication here is that reality does not resist belief; rather, it bends to fit it.

Final Remark: The Future of Human Beliefs

If collective belief is the invisible force that makes up a civilization, then the next evolution of humanity will be those who learn to control, reshape, and elevate beliefs beyond that which exists today.

Are we still to remain trapped in cycles of dog-fighting ideology?

Or will we release this interconnected consciousness into its truest full expression?

The answer does not lie in what we know-but rather what we believe.

Chapter 11: The Concept of Free Will: Believism's Challenge to Determinism

---

The Beginning of the Free Will Debate: First Schooled Philosophers Who Stood Up for Freedom

• Free will was debated among philosophers before science, religion, and psychology entered into especially ancient civilizations.

• **Ancient Egyptians:** Fate, as believed, is written by the gods in the sense of "heka," or divine magic, that enabled human beings to re-make destiny.

• **Hinduism & Karma:** Free will reigned because hapless souls could choose not to suffer the consequences of their bad actions. In other words, there was hope to improve karma through choices made in the life to come.

• **Socrates vs. Fate:** Knowledge of oneself is, therefore, the very basis for making one's own choices, and it is, therefore, ignorance rather than fate or destiny that governs mankind.

The battle between free will and determinism dates back to stuff that was a good deal earlier than science took form; what has changed?

But there is a Problem of Free Will in Christianity, Islam, and Buddhism Religions tried to put forth an answer to this dilemma: if God is omniscient, does it not follow that everything is predetermined?

The Rift in Christianity:

• Calvinists maintain that free will is an illusion—God already knows everything you will do.

• Catholics maintained free will must exist; otherwise morality doesn't mean anything.

Debate Between Qadar and Free Will in Islam:

• Some Muslim theologians believe Allah has determined everything (fatalism).

• Others would say that humans possess some free will, but only within the grand design of God.

Buddhism's Radical Perspective:

• Detachment from oneself implies no self exists to have free will. Choices do exist; however, the self illusory—who makes the choice, then?

Even religions could not unravel the paradox of free will.

The Modern Science Assessment: Are We Just Complex Machines?

Free will is being denounced by neuroscience, genetics, and psychology:

• **Neuroscience:** Scan the brain, and it shows that decisions are made even before awareness cluttered them.

• **Genetics:** Studies reveal that 40-50% of personality can be genetically transmitted; therefore, many choices can be biologically predetermined.

• **Psychology:** External stimuli exert considerable influence on our choices.

If all this is true, do we really make any decisions?

Is there still a possibility of escape?

Carl Jung describes the shadow self as the unconscious mind that controls much of our behavior.

• People think they make rational decisions, but most are made amid hidden emotions, past traumas, and instincts.

• Studies have found that 90% of one's daily actions occur unconsciously and habitually.

• Even creativity, which often seems spontaneous, can oftentimes be just the subconscious mind solving problems in the background.

If most of the brain's functions are unconsciously directed towards the planning, regulating, etc., of our decision-making powers, free will becomes but a figment.

Or can we learn to control the shadow?

Free Will and the Unconscious: Can You Reprogram Your Brain?

Could it be that the unconscious mind is not a prison but a tool that can be molded and designed?

• **Cognitive Behavioral Therapy (CBT):** Can boost the rewiring of habits in one's unconscious thought patterns.

• **Hypnosis:** Can eliminate the bad habits, modify fears, and facilitate a change in perception regarding pain.

• **Neuroplasticity:** The system permits physical rewiring of the brain as per the scopes of focus.

So, if the unconscious can be hacked, trained, and transformed, does free will actually exist after all?

• **Chaos Factor:** The Butterfly Effect and Why Small Choices Matter. Determinism assumes that if the universe were pushed backward and played again, everything would happen just like it did before.

But theory of chaos dictates otherwise:

• **The Butterfly Effect:** Infinitesimals (like that of a butterfly flapping its wings) can lead to profoundly different futures.

• **Weather Systems:** Impossible to predict beyond a certain period since small factors spiral into chaos.

• **Brain Complexity:** The human brain has over 86 billion neurons-so complicated that a small change is enough to reshape a decision altogether.

Maybe, then, because small inputs can induce large changes, free will could exist amidst this chaos.

5. The Psychology of Rebellion: Why Do Some People Resist Control, while Others Don't

In some historical periods, people obeyed authority unchallenged while others defied at all costs.

Milgram's Experiment: In the year 1961, it was shown that 65% will obey authority even at the expense of injuring others.

The Stanford Prison Experiment: Authority quickly became abusive, while subjects put in a subordinate situation quickly turned passive.

Revolutions: Every great revolution began with a few individuals rejecting acceptance of "fate." The explanation of rebellion, resistance, and defiance, if free will is nonexistent.

Memory determines choices, and do they still belong to meer?

Memories lead to decisions, whose truthfulness is elusive.

Every recollection, each time, is created anew-meaning your past is quite unstable.

"Trauma, nostalgia, and childhood experiences create your identity, dictate your choices in ways you don't control."

If actions were completely set free by the past, it doesn't mean belief in free will would exist.

Erasing fate by changing memories. What if we could change memories that give free will?

Rewriting memory: A few psychologists believe if you can alter your memories, you may behave differently around painful experiences.

Dummy memories: Behavioral scientists have implanted false memories, thereby demonstrating, if only in part, that "reality" is pliable.

This observably does not bear out well for the so-called, Mandela effect-to a large group of persons who essentially hold seemingly divergent views.

It means both memory can be rewritten and free will allowing self-directioning so that any memory may be divined for oneself.

Genetic Engineering When Your dna Decides for You

As science approaches the future gene-editing technologies, shall we be soon engineering choices anyway?

CRISPR Technology: As science puts it, engineers intelligence, personality, and moral behavior before birth.

Eugenics 2.0: If society takes it on, determining the people with pre-given characteristics, is the space for free will squeezed?

Neuro-enhancements: Implants in the brain and medication-potentially augmentive cognitive enhancement-whence the cost?

If genetic modification is choreographing our future, then has the world met the kind of world in which "choice" is anathema?

Cognitive Disobedience: Why We Will Never Admit We Are Not in Control

The mind abhors contradiction, and it builds upon illusions to provide a certain stability:

Studies show that people typically rationalize their actions after, rather than before, engaging in them, leading them to conclude that oftentimes it seems they act and then justify later that they did so.

The "I Meant to Do That" fallacy-people tell themselves that they were in control, even when they weren't.

Religious and political beliefs: They are often defended, not because they are true, but simply from the irreversible decision of the mind against perceiving itself as wrong.

If humans obfuscate with fictive illusions the notion of free will, is it simply a lie with which we are comfortable?

The Split-Brain Experiments: Evidence That Says "You" Aren't Always in Control

Something astonishing occurred after the severing of the fibers connecting the two hemispheres of the brain in 1961:

The left hand began moving as if against its own conscious intention.

Such patients invented stories to justify their actions-an example that proves we fabricate our motives for doing things we did not control.

While, your conscious mind has no free tamper; in most other cases, decisions are made unconsciously and unrecognized.

If even the brain cannot differentiate between left and right, is it still possible to say you decide alone?

The Rebellion Against Control-Hacking The System Back To Reclaiming Choice

If we still live in a deterministic world, then we can still rebel for our own stamp of freedom.

Knowing this, that awareness is the power in you: first the knowledge helps with free will about how some certain systems control you.

Strategic rebellion: The defiance, whether resisting algorithms or questioning social norms, polarizes action about breaking the disturbing cycles of predictable determinism.

Self-programming: Neuroplasticity, memory work, and perception hacking allow you to break deep down into the average level, mapping your thoughts and behavior patterns anew.

The last free will comes in the choice to fight for it.

Free Will as a Surviving Mechanism

Evolution has developed to embody some adaptable forms and fit forms; what if free will were an illusion acknowledged by evolution, as it shores up efforts to survive?

The free will is not to be treated as to indicate that an animal has it; rather, the animal responds immediately by instinct and has the savage knowledge of survival.

In the opinion of the functions of the human brain, the arguments are put forth for a diverse prospectus-this precautionary feature should allow superiority.

Whatever advanced predictive-making activity has to take places behind the ordinary stereotypic behavior of free will is felt and said to be present.

At this point, free will raises the very excited question: If free will were but an illusion produced by an evolution to give us the torchlight of control, it stands to imply, then, that we were never free.

The Social Benefit of Free Will: The Great Myth That Keeps Society Together

A belief in acceptance and autonomy would, in precept, enhance the overall effectiveness of the running society.

Without belief in free will-the general consensus, crime and chaos would be the outcome, having no basis for accountability on which society holds the mean of bonds.

Religion, ethics, and laws enshrine a certain fallacious lust-the free will that allows its practitioners to have some real choices.

It is thus a matter of a complete mustiam-into obedience-when at the end so betide that there exists no such free will. It means, in other words, we've got to end up believing it, whatever the case may be.

The DNA Dictatorship: How Your Genes Choose for You

Genes differ very little from computer programming in the way they set personality, preferences, and habits in human beings.

What behavior genetics settles is that much of what you are has been manufactured even before your birth.

Some studies show that

most habits, personality, desire development, risk taking, intelligence, political beliefs present their genesis in genes;

hereditarily endowed cognitive characteristics play the greatest role in such: addiction, aggression, and emotional expression.

In a word: If your propensities are determined by genetics, just how much of you really is you?

If those instructions coded in your genes begin to make decisions on your behalf, "free will" is little more than a construct of biology.

The Hormonal Hijack: How Chemicals Control Your Choices

Your desire is mediated by the dopamine system.

Your serotionin system executes your pleasure drive.

Your cortisol affects how stressed out you might get.

Chemicals influence essentially every choice you make-such as which food to eat and with whom to fall in love.

This means: Your body is making choices before your mind does.

The idea of free will that you hold comes directly from the neurochemical activity taking place in your brain.

So, the example just mentioned doesn't really justify "free will" at all, while brain chemistry dictates how we feel, think, and subsequently act.

Free Will Politics: Does Society Want You To Think You Have It?

Belief in free will is used as a political instrument by governments, religions, and corporations in the following ways:

Democracy is based on free will; without free choice, democracy is meaningless.

Capitalism sells choice; companies market this illusory 'freedom': But are your choices really yours or simply the result of marketing?

Dictatorial beliefs "limit" free will: Under authoritarianism, the dictator will claim to control fate itself, citing denial of free will as a justification for authority.

However, if "free will" is viewed as a political stance, consequently, it would determine the very structure of a society.

The Lopez of Consumer Choice: Are your choices your choices or choice conditioning?

Capitalism has to move forward under the assumption of choice and free will, but are you really free to want what you want?

He used psychology to make the masses desire products without having any notion that it was being done to them (Edward Bernays: The Father of Propaganda).

Choice Architecture Control: A store, advertisement, or application is designed in such a way that it silently directs your behavior while you are under the false pretense that you have made a free choice.

Social Conditioning: Trends aren't organic; they're engineered and "foisted" upon you. Market forces and cultural programming account for the expansive majority of your "free choices."

If your desires aren't your own, can you say you're free?

Wage Slave Paradox: If You Choose to Work, Are You Free?

In the capitalist sector, it is often said by them that individuals happen to choose between working for themselves; although, this doesn't mean a total truth.

No Work = No Survival: If you need money to live with, is working really a choice, or is it under force from the economy?

`9-to-5` lockdown: When they were at work, engineers-so busy-did not seek to ask what chains were placed on them.

"Self-Made" Myth: The billionaires in every way fed their life off of governmental money, inherited privileges, and systemic advantages.

So if the only way out for one is through that beaten yet predictable path, wherein lies free will?

To your grand illusion-how society programs your choices:

Even when everyone confirms free will is something facing the individual, how come it is not limited to a sword inside one's sheath?

The governments, corporations, and institutions decide the choices which other people supposedly have before them.

It is an illusion of freedom of choice, sustained via:

The control over information that reaches you-one of the finest art;

Manipulation of the economy in a way that some choices become harder or easier to take;

Social engineering through valorizing the values that you adopted.

If choices are merely the result of external influences out of control, are you really free?

Manufactured Consent: The Free Will Paradox of Democracy

Democracy is built on the premise of free will, yet what if it were a deception, however sophisticated?

Chomsky offers an answer of "manufactured consent." He believes that the ordinary citizenry are somewhat duped into believing that choice is made in the actions of government upon public consent and free will when there is actually a whole range of manipulations.

If you are a regular politician nowadays:

You present the candidate;

The media creates the environment;

You entice a populace into choices they normally would not accept;

Putting these together, what this gives you is a range of options from which you have to pick. In that circumstance, that is entirely about free will, isn't it?

So if free will is real, how do so many humans come to a monotonous same kind of decision in the end?

Quantum Indeterminacy: The Universe Is Not Fully Determined

Newton's laws suggested a clockwork universe; quantum took train of thought and pulled its tracks off.

• Particles do not go by strict rules; they act assuming probabilities.

• The wave function has collapsed in the sense that, upon the act of observing, reality changes, and thus the observer has influenced reality.

• Quantum decisiveness: Some physicists have begun to think of consciousness playing a role in querying quantum outcomes.

How can one say that what we choose is determined, given this universe is not fully, but somewhat determined?

The paradox of free will: the final verdict by the believers.

Accordingly, free will can be real or an illusion-it makes no difference.

Because

The moment that you choose to believe in this or that free will, you act as though this was true; and if actions create reality, then believing in free will creates it.

Will is not a gift to be given, free will is chosen.

Schrödinger's free will: Are we in a superposition of choices, or choices?

Quantum mechanics stands in stark contradiction to the idea of determinism with an innate sense of antipathy from its father's old physics.

Because in classical physics, there will always be some law that must be followed. Photons will be in a state of superposition except when they are measured in quantum physics.

Simply by observing a phenomenon, the double-slit experiment changes the very fabric of reality. Is it a huge question whether perception and consciousness are engaged in establishing the actual angle of future reality?

If reality itself is uncertain until time is observed, where does free will sit in the framework?

Theories of the Many-World Hypothesis: Are All Your Choices Made in Parallel Universes?

According to quantum theory, every possible choice spawns a different universe.

Thus, at the given point, there are an infinite number of lives of you, each making a certain choice and living a different life.

The whole thing begins to get a little unsettling:

But that brings up the concern. If every single choice does exist somewhere, how can there be free will?

Another, also less commonly offered alternative is, could it just be that I am experiencing only one out of infinite alternate lives? Now, if free wit is only truly there because all choices are made elsewhere, do we indeed have it or not?

AI's Impact on Decision-Making

AI develops predictions and instills choices no mere human rationale can fathom:

Before making input decision, algorithms are already predicting what you will want to buy or watch or even perceive. AI acts on behalf of political campaigners to sway voters into believing they've made independent choices. The feeds of social media trap you in an affirmational loop designed to hijack attention and reinforce belief.

So, does this ability of AI to foresee and drive your decisions nullify free will?

Algorithmic free will: can AI have consciousness and choice?

At this moment, AI is already providing us with the choice of what to watch and what to buy.

If it learns and adapts, does that in essence mean that it's developing its own sort of free will?

Some scientists, justifiably, propose that consciousness arises from complexity; thus far, a super-advanced AI will eventually become self-aware with real decision-making.

Does that mean that if AI can have free will, we are just biological machines carrying out some advanced algorithm?

AI is basically telling us how to conduct our lives now, without our conscious awareness of it.

AI controls the media, along with the news and ads, nudging us towards decisions that, in most cases, we aren't aware we're making.

With the unimaginable power through AI managing our lives will it be just a matter of time before it decides for us-how dare it take away the power we each have to decide?

Yet another danger: Is AI going to imprison us without chains? Indirectly, it is on the verge of taking our freedom of choice away.

The Simulation Hypothesis: Are We Nothing More than Code?

If the universe were indeed a computer simulation, then everything in it-including free will-would simply be code.

Physicists such as Nick Bostrom argue that perhaps we are actually living in a massively advanced computer simulation.

If the reality itself is predetermined by an external system, does free will exist in that reality?

Attention as Currency: Who Holds Your Will?

Attention is the currency of free will. Whoever controls your focus controls your choices.

Big Tech has hacked human psychology.

Infinite scroll, dopamine loops, notification triggers; all to decide for you.

Every second spent reacting rather than acting amounts to your free will being handed over to someone else.

To take back your will,

you must reclaim your attention.

The question is: Can you?

The Algorithmic Cage: AI and the Death of Free Will

AI literally decides what you see, read, and believe every day.

These recommender algorithms on social media, YouTube, and Netflix do not merely provide suggestions based on what you might want; they actively shape what you will eventually come to want.

It creates an atmosphere of self-reinforcing echo chambers:

You think you are choosing what to consume while in reality, the AI is shaping your tastes before you ever begin your choice-making process.

If AI can predict the next thing you will do even before you do it, is that a choice at all?

Become the Architect of Your Mind

Let free will be an illusion, provided that one can hack down the system.

The secret lies in metacognition- thinking about thinking.

You will have to establish:

The invisible forces behind your choices.

Reprogram your habits, beliefs, and mental models.

Build an individual philosophy against that of society inherited from you.

True freedom is not to mean full freedom, but pertains to the mastery over the game of bondage.

Key-ediction: Yielding to Destiny or forgoing it.

Two options sheet out before you:

1. **Accept determinism:** firmly embrace the thinking, the philosophy that you are anomalously set in within yourself as mere units of preconditioning by physics, biology, and history.

2. **Defy fate:** from your perspective, do as you please, irrespective of what the Universe throws at you.

The greatest belief is that, all things considered, your actions do, one or another, really matter.

Because when it's all said and done, reality is what goes for those who think they can change it.

Chapter 12: The Evolution of Belief: From Survival to Enlightenment

Beyond Transcendence: The Next Phase of Human Evolution

It is belief which is the bedrock upon which walk the absorbent footsteps of modern-day civilization. It has mobilized every war, erected every empire, quelled every revolution, and inspired every discovery. But where does it lead from here?

Belief has taken on the form dictated by the forces of survival, power, and control throughout millennia of human existence. Guided now by different underlying principles, as the transition to a New Age becomes apparent, belief does not relate to mere survival anymore but has now become a yearning for transcendence.

Transcendence does not mean escaping from the material world but, rather, reformatting the very way we experience existence.

1. Neurobiology of Belief: How the Brain Constructs Reality

At the core of belief lies the brain - the engine of perception capable of turning the abstract into physical reality.

How Belief Is Created by the Brain?

Neuroscience shows that belief is not just an idea but a vast network of neurons wired together through repetition and reinforcement.

Neuroplasticity: The brain is subject to continuous rewiring, which means that what we believe today is not a fixed commodity; it has room to be reshaped.

The Limbic System: This emotional core of the brain determines what we feel sacred about. When our limbic system is overwhelmed by a belief to the point of conviction, the flood of neurotransmitters makes that belief feel more real than reality itself.

The Prefrontal Cortex: That's where the higher reasoning takes place, where we can verify or refute existing beliefs.

When a belief is strongly entrenched, it is physically wired into the brain. That is why changing a belief can often feel akin to breaking from an addiction-it can be neurologically painful.

However, if we want to hijack belief-making mechanisms, it is possible. We can reprogram our minds.

2. The Cognitive Revolution: When Belief Became Power

For a long period, the lives of humans were marked as almost primitive, remembering a time when they were mere hunter-gatherers, governed by their instincts and by immediate needs. Something, however, shifted with the Cognitive Revolution, which began around some 70,000 years back.

Humans unlocked the imaginatory power of a soul–the power of believing wholeheartedly in things that did not eventually exist.

Believing in gods created and fostered the idea of religions.

Believing in tribes, larger ones and the idea of nations.

Believing in currency took the form of economies.

None of these things exist in nature. They exist only in the mind.

It was the most significant gain in terms of human evolution; it became possible to invent reality by shared belief.

Today, we take them to be beyond question, mere stories we, as a group, accept as a reality.

The Cognitive Revolution demonstrated one thing:

Whoever controls belief, controls the world.

3. The Ideological Wars: When Belief Became a Weapon

From the moment they realized that belief could shape the world, the war for belief broke out.

Religion fought for souls.

Empire fought for ideology.

Politic systems fought for narratives.

Each war in history is one of belief, and each revolution is a struggle between old and new ideologies.

An empire collapses when faith in the divine authority of the ruling becomes extinct.

The USSR sank down when the funds for its belief in communism were withdrawn.

In this sense, every dictatorship in history has been about simply framing citizens in such a belief system that puts the dictator before all others.

The real battle is not a force that uses weapons; it is fought with a mind.

Even in the present day, the greatest struggles of our era are wars of belief:

Democracy versus Authoritarianism

Globalism against Nationalism

Science against Conspiracy

The future belongs to those who win the war of belief.

4. The Evolution of Spirituality: From Gods to Self-Actualization

Religions exercised their power over human civilization at many times militias. But gradually they evolved belief systems:

1. Polytheism: The initial appointment of many gods by early humans served to bring order into the nihilism of nature.

2. Monotheism: Power over each society is crushed under the will of One, mirroring sorely and directly the political hierarchy of powers in society.

3. Scientific Rationalism: That power of involves lean very much toward an Enlightenment thinking that believed in the unquestionable opportunities braced on reason and empirical evidence.

4. New age and self-spirituality: Today, it is an internalized and self-formed belief system-own interpretation creating meaning that mix science, psychology as well as spirit.

It should be said non-death of belief: rather, it speaks about evolution.

Where do people even go about creating a belief system anymore?

Humankind transcends beyond its external god and emerges upward as a divine force.

5. The Age of Artificial Belief: Can Machines Have Faith?

Now, humanity is opening a new chapter called AI, consciousness and machine-intelligence.

If belief gives rise to reality, while AI starts getting independent thoughts, then:

Will AI ever "believe" in anything really of its own?

Will AI challenge the human notion of reality with completely different perspectives?

Will AI create religions and belief systems for itself?

A land unexplored.

For the first time, belief is outside the boundary of the human brain.

When machines are able to believe, what would that say about our reality for the future?

6. The Paradox of Free Thought: Can We Escape Our Own Beliefs?

Belief defines reality.

But does that mean we are trapped in the space of our belief system?

The greatest paradox of human existence is this:

More you believe in something, the more real it becomes.

But that means also quote the other way around:

The only way to evolve is to oppose what is believed.

But what if all you believe is wrong?

What if reality is far greater than can be perceived right now?

What if the limits you are experiencing are there just because you believe it's there?

History has sadly shown us that those who oppose belief systems become the change of the world.

Galileo opposed the view of Earth-Middle of the Universe.

Einstein opposed the concept of absolute time.

Human history has from the other hand shown us that those who oppose this class who control power.

And now it is our own turn to oppose belief.

Because the last frontier of evolution is not physical-it is mental.

7. Cognitive Singularity: Where Belief Becomes Self-Aware

In its passage through history, belief has been the progressive force of humanity, but there comes a point where belief itself evolves to the point of being self-aware, a moment referred to as the Cognitive Singularity that is where humans see belief as a tool and a limitation.

This is the place where psychology, neuroscience, and philosophy come together. The brain, composed of interlinked wrappings of 86 billion neurons, is not simply for processing; it generates interpretations that construct and truly believes in realities. Evolutionarily, beliefs were survival mechanisms. But today, those mechanisms aid in self-definition. Then what happens when we actually start believing in belief itself? When we consciously float our mental frameworks with the full awareness that they are not solid structures but malleable constructs?

This is the intersection moment of cognitive self-awareness-it is the path to recognizing the very essence that belief is software in operation on the hardware of the brain. The transition from instinctual belief to self-directed belief is parallel to that of evolution from unconsciousness to a conscious technologically-driven process. On the cusp of humanity itself, at the threshold of its systems of beliefs, made to question, rewrite, and eventually transcend belief systems, this is an age of conflict.

8. The neuroscience of self-directed evolution means hacking the mind.

If belief is the software, can we hack the software? What neuroscientists have discovered, to the great relief of everyone who seeks to change their lives, is that brain plasticity allows the brain to rewire itself with experience and intention. This is called neuroplasticity, and it shows that belief is more than just passive acceptance of reality; it creates reality by changing brain circuitry.

What is mind-blowing, however, is this: experiments involving neurofeedback, psychedelics, and meditation reveal that it is humans who consciously edit their beliefs. Monks that were scanned via fMRI while in deep meditation show the default mode network, the system responsible for the self-construct, being actively suppressed. In effect, they are erasing their own belief structures, proving identity itself to be malleable.

Then, here comes the evolutionary question: what if humanity learned to actually rewire beliefs in mass? What if conscious evolution replaced biological evolution? Given a beatific brain in a mind set for infinite possibilities, are there limits left?

Believism in its highest form is not just individual transformation that transforms someone's life; it's hacking reality itself through neurobiological self-evolution.

9. Memetic Evolution: The Survival of Ideas Over Genes

Just like Darwinian evolution normally used genes as its point of departure, Dawkins elaborated memes: the unit of cultural information that evolves in a way reminiscent of biological life. Memetic evolution is faster than genetic evolution in the age of digital technology.

Religions, ideologies, political movements, scientific breakthroughs—competent memetic structures competing for survival. Entry into the memetic realm occurs in minutes, while entry into the genetic realm occurs over millennia. Systems of beliefs, therefore, are evolving rapidly at an infinitely increasing pace.

What does this mean: If, in the 20th century, there were two revolutions in ideologies, the question arises: what can be expected in the next one hundred years? The entire belief system landscape may mutate beyond recognition. This, in fact, constitutes an opportunity and a risk—when belief systems evolve so fast that human psychology cannot really catch up.

Memetic selection will be the next dominant belief structures. Some ideas will survive while others fade away. The battle for the future of human consciousness is happening right now in the information wars of the twenty-first century.

10. The Singularity of Thought: Where AI and Human Understanding Meet

Now more than ever, AI has crossed frontiers in becoming the creator of human belief. Algorithms determine what we see, what we learn, even what we believe to be real. If belief be the basis of human experience and AI has taken art as the controller of belief, what shall happen when AI becomes the architect of reality?

We stand at the edge of a precipice-the Singularity of Thought-a point in history when human cognition ceases to be separated from artificial intelligence. AI is already encoding itself deep within the collective subconscious of an otherwise independent and self-governing populace. Social media, recommendation algorithms, deepfake technology-they're no longer just tools. They mimesis-engineer, creating the beliefs of entire populations.

If belief is the most potent force that shapes human destiny, who controls the architects of belief? To those who control the mechanisms of creating belief, power of the future will belong in their hands.

Then shall free thought be a goose-notion, existing only as myth in the age of AI? Or indeed is this a chance for humanity to consciously gain control of its belief systems while they still can, so-named by AI?

11. The Death of Objective Reality: Living in the Post-Truth Era

For most of history, humans sought objective truth—scientific facts, empirical data, universal principles. But today, truth itself is fragmenting. In the post-truth era, belief determines reality more than facts.

Philosophers have long debated whether there even exists such a thing as objective truth and, having departed from philosophy, this debate is now creeping into geopolitics, technology, and society. Rather than conventional forms of knowledge, conspiracy theories, ideological echo chambers, and digital illusions on the Internet have emerged. Individuals do not believe what is true; they believe what meets their predestined mental setups.

This raises the ultimate question: If reality is now completely subjective, can truth survive? Or has humanity entered in a new age, totally guided by belief? Militarily, this defines the moment when the builder of belief will assume total power over the rest.

13. The Psychological Cost of Infinite Belief: When Everything is Possible, What is Real?

Historically, the force of belief has been humankind's greatest strength-however, what comes after when belief becomes an element that cannot be constrained? Where does the human mind fix some stability when belief becomes a determining act with regard to what is real?

This is the paradox of cognitive infinity-wherein the mind in a neurological state is aware of infinite possible realities, yet cannot stand stable on any one of those realities. There is philosophical consideration that too much freedom leads to paralysis, defining existential paralysis, a state in which within buildings exists a vacuum of belief-a situation where nothing feels real.

But structure would keep things together. The hyper-reality, as Les Fleurs du Mal's great philosopher Jean Baudrillard spoke about, is that situation where reality is overturned by simulations; where one cannot differentiate between what is real and what is constructed.

Can purposefully constructed belief form the basis for a way of life, or does the mind require some limits with which to survive? Therein lies the dichotomy: the liberation of the mind against cognitive chaos.

Evolution is no longer about extension of beliefs; neither is it the end of world-hopping-it's about learning how best to control them without losing touch with what we call reality.

14. The Illusion of the Individual: Are We Truly Separate, or Just Splinters of a Greater Mind?

If belief creates reality, then the self is merely an illusion—an illusion strengthened by human perception. What if individuality is itself a false construct?

The idea of separateness is a relatively modern concept in human history. Early civilizations saw themselves as part of a united whole. Tribes and spiritual constraints: shared destiny were more common. The modern sense of individualism began to emerge only in the Renaissance, and even later in the Enlightenment time. But even now, neuroscience is throwing the older constructs into doubt, wondering if the very existence of individuality is correct.

Research on split-brain patients indicates that within one person, there can be multiple forms of consciousness. The disconnection focusses on the corpus callosum dysfunction of either the left or right hemispheres: each hemisphere acts as an individual entity. Formally, therefore, consciousness is not static, not a blank page with fixed boundaries that distinguishes one human being from another; instead, it's fluid and on the move.

If belief creates the self, workable belief is thus a construct, with identity obviously adaptable-not a reality. After all, if all minds are connected, wherein lies that separation we see, but survival itself-a mere evolutionary ruse.

Belief in self may be the final illusion mankind is to outgrow.

15. The Collapse of Linear Time: Does Belief Extend Beyond the Present?

We experience time as linear, but this is simply a limitation of cognition and not a reality. The brain has constructed the past- present-future continuum, leading a few physicists and neuroscientists to conclude that time is not objective reality but rather an interpretation rendered by the brain.

The idea is corroborated by quantum mechanics. A number of experiments, statements one example: the double-slit experiment, assert that upon observation, a particle's behavior changes, thus making it possible for the future to influence the past. If the physical universe operates outside of time, does belief have the power to shape not merely the future but also the past itself?

Time has come to be seen as an illusion imposed by the mind since ancient spiritual traditions, from Hinduism to Buddhism, have been saying so. But does modern science only begin to catch up?

This brings forth an altogether new path: if belief is time-less, then memory, identity, even history itself, is subject to the power of belief.

The Algorithmic Gods: When AI becomes the dark architects of credence

Belief has transitioned from an organic process to an engineered process for the first time in history. The architect of belief is no longer slated on ideologies formed by religion, the church, or philosophers-but by artificial intelligence.

The algorithms that are in place to direct the digital world-the social media, the newsfeeds, the recommendation systems-are not neutral; they filter select parts of publics' viewpoints, which in turn creates their beliefs about either others or the world. It is no longer money, nor military might that is the most powerful force in the world today-it is control over belief formation.

But what happens when the artificial intelligence surpasses cognition? What happens when prediction algorithms present what people will believe faster than opinions are formed? The Singularity of Thought is no longer abstract-it is actively being created.

If belief generates a decided reality, and AI believes that, then AI's future is but the architect of reality itself.

The question is: Will humanity allow itself to design its belief structure, or will it become denominantly a prisoner to an artificial belief matrix?

17. The Belief Singularity: When Humanity Becomes Its Own God

If belief shapes reality, and humanity reaches a state where belief is fully self-directed, then what happens?

This is the final stage: The Belief Singularity—where humanity has absolute control over its own existence. At this stage, limitations cease to exist, and reality becomes a conscious construct.

Philosophically, this is what some religious traditions have hinted at—divinity as not a being, but a state of consciousness. The idea that God is simply the point where consciousness fully recognizes its own creative power.

This raises the ultimate question: If we have the power to shape all reality, what will we choose to create?

Because belief is no longer just a tool—it is the ultimate force of existence.

18. Quantum Mind: Do Thoughts Exist Outside the Brain?

For centuries, science treated consciousness as a byproduct of the brain: a bunch of chemical and electrical reactions going on in the skull. But what if that premise is untrue?

Quantum mechanics points to a deep entwinement between consciousness and the material world. The observer effect shows us that whatever behavior a particle will exhibit is dependent on whether a conscious being wants to look for it, implying that perception changes physical reality. Some researchers in recent years have proposed that consciousness is not limited to the brain at all, but exists as a field, much like gravity or electromagnetism.

If true, belief exists not only internally but also in some way in communication with reality. The human mind is potentially a receiver and a transmitter of reality, not only a creator of thoughts in isolation.

It means that our thoughts, feelings, and beliefs could exist outside of ourselves: could thereby persist beyond death, could create the physical universe, and could connect all human minds into a single network of consciousness.

If belief is not merely internal, but an energetic force, then what we believe may not only shape our lives but even the very fabric of reality itself.

19. The Dark Side of Belief: Can We Create Our Own Demons?

If belief creates reality, then what happens when belief is corrupted?

Myths, legends, and religions have spoken of evil entities—demons, djinn, malevolent spirits. But what if these were not inherent in reality? Instead, they are manifestations of belief in itself.

The concept of tulpas, perhaps originating from Tibetan mysticism, suggests that focused thought can sometimes create independent entities. Various researchers believe that mass hysteria, fear, or simply collective paranoia have the power to bring thought-forms into being.

If enough people believe something, does it exist on an energetic plane outside of us?

This, in turn, brings with it a dreadful idea: that every fear humankind has ever harbored has, somehow, merged into reality. The more we believe in darkness, the more real it becomes.

If belief is limitless, then humanity's ultimate question must be: are we creating our own monsters, and if so, will we be able to unmake them?

20. The War for Reality - who Controls What You Believe?

Beliefs shape the world; therefore, whoever controls beliefs possesses the most power to influence the entire universe.

Governments, religions, and institutions have, throughout history, fought to control what people believe. From the ancient empires to the modern propaganda, the battle has always been waged on determining who gets to decide what is real.

But in centuries past, the war has taken a new height.

Social media algorithms send messages in a way that one believes unaware.

Deepfake software can be able to create a reality.

AI-designed narratives can create a whole system of belief in all precision.

A dangerous idea is not in who controls power-the question is: who controls belief itself?

If a person's very belief is their world, then to control belief is the same as controlling reality. The ultimate war now rages not with weapons but with ideas.

So, are you controlling your beliefs, or are your beliefs being controlled for you?

21. The Grand Simulation: Is Reality Another Belief?

What if everything is just not an objective reality, but a belief system so entrenched that we actually believe the same to be true?

The Simulation Hypothesis argues on account of a high-order intelligence, as in the form of a very complicated simulated universe-a digital reality created by some higher intelligence. What would happen if it were mental instead of technological?

We assume that the universe works in harmony with laws-but what if these laws exist at all because we think they do?

We think of time as linear-but what if time is just an illusion created by human consciousness?

We think of ourselves as individual-but what if we are just tiny fragments of a larger consciousness, experiencing itself in different forms?

If reality is shaped by belief, then belief itself is the true architecture of existence.

22. Death of Consensus Reality: Are We Heading Towards a Multiverse of Minds?

In past ages, humans lived and acted in a single living framework- religion, cultures, traditions welded whole civilizations together. But now, society is fragmenting.

Some people believe in science; others believe in spirituality.

Some believe the Earth is round; others think that it's flat.

Some believe in some external reality; others subscribe to the idea that we create it.

With increasing individualization of the belief systems, we may well witness the death of the single shared reality.

But if belief makes reality, and if conflicting beliefs live within different people, does it follow from this that multiple realities are now co-existing?

This raised a shocking possibility; humanity does not inhabit one universe, but the multiverse of minds: where different people literally occupy different versions of reality based on what they believe.

If that is the case, the future is the opposite of one shared world; instead, there are diverging infinite realities based on belief.

23. Beyond Humanity: What Happens When We Outgrow Our Own Existence?

If belief gives shape to reality and if belief ever reaches a stage where we shall finally have mastered it, does that make us less human?

Would we then refer to ourselves as humans, or should we transcend these organic boundaries?

From Nietzsche to transhumanists, the greatest of philosophers have argued that humanity is not the end point; it is rather a transition.

The realm beyond belief is neither mere enlightenment nor transcendence; it is evolution.

A reality where:

Thought creates matter.

Consciousness is unrestricted by time.

Individual identity becomes continuous with universal intelligence.

If belief knows no boundaries, then framed only by the work of our imaginations are we.

Conclusion: One Final Choice: What Will You Believe?

This is our grand finale.

Everything we have discussed brings us down to one last fact:

There is no reality.

There is only belief.

The universe is not a spectator sport; it is not something you observe but something you make.

The relevant query is no longer, what is truth?

The question is:

What will you choose to believe?

For surely, whatever you believe...

That is where reality will be.

Chapter 13: Belief and the Universe: The Mind's Role in the Cosmic Tapestry

#1. The Cosmic Observer: Does Consciousness Create the Universe?

The Fundamental Paradox of Matter, Mind and Universe

For millennia, mankind has accepted that the universe exists in all its dimension beyond mankind, and that space, time, and matter appear as objective entities dancing along in the great cosmic orchestra of precise rules. What if we were wrong in our assumptions of this nature? What if the conscious mind of the observer itself forms the reality as opposed to a passive one awaiting discovery?

This idea can no longer be considered purely mystical or philosophical. Contemporary physics has put forth possible cracks in the structure of materialism, suggesting a much more active role of consciousness in the shaping of material reality. Quantum mechanics-the very science of the microscopic world-has proposed a rather unnerving but tantalizing idea: the universe has no definite state until it has been observed.

Take, for example, the celebrated double-slit experiment, in which a particle will display the characteristics of a wave existing in several places simultaneously until measured. It is only on measurement that one observer-as if holding a giant hand-gestures and determines the wave to retake its former shape in becoming a certain point of reality, and observation itself has determined the different outcome. This awakens the more disturbing question: if reality is determined by observation, what was the nature of the universe prior to the first conscious observer?

The Observer Problem: Who Watches the Watcher?

If it is true that it is consciousness bringing reality into play; did the first observer see the universe into being? Or was a cosmic mind responsible for making reality unfold? This accords with the ancient spiritual and philosophical traditions, which assert that the universe is ever that thought, a dream, or itself a simulation of consciousness.

The Upanishads speak of Brahman, an infinite consciousness dreaming the universe into being. Taoism describes the Tao, the unformed force which flows within all existence. And even modern thoughts see a participatory universe, promoted by thinkers such as John Wheeler, who worked beside Einstein. According to this view, reality is not a passive configuration but an entity that depends on observation for it to take shape into reality.

But would this mean, for example, that if reality is to be observer-dependent, then how did the first observer emerge? A cosmic intelligence? The self-aware force itself embedded in the fabric of the universe? Or does this very question put us into an infinite loop-an eternal recursion where the observer and the observed give birth to each other?

Beyond Materialism: The Death of Objective Reality

If consciousness creates reality, then the notion of a purely physical world collapses. We can no longer say that atoms, stars, galaxies, and black holes exist in some absolute sense. Instead, we must confront the possibility that existence itself is a construct of perception-an interface designed to shape experience rather than represent an external, independent world.

This idea destroys classical science. A materialist view holds that the brain functions to generate consciousness just as any mechanical object generates heat. But if reality is shaped by consciousness, then the brain is not the producer of awareness; rather, it is a sort of receiver, a conduit through which a greater field of consciousness interacts with what we perceive as reality.

This coincides with what Donald Hoffman, a cognitive scientist, proposes in his G_Interface Theory of Perception_. He argues, according to the G_Interface Theory of Perception, that space, time, and objects are not fundamental, but only symbols devised by our minds to facilitate navigation through a deeper, hidden reality. Just as a computer desktop presents icons rather than exposing raw electrical signals, our senses furnish a filtered and simplified version of a much bigger truth.

The Cosmic Mind: Are We Norms of a More Extensive Intelligence?

If perception shapes reality, and if our minds serve as receivers of consciousness rather than its creators, then we must ask ourselves: do we belong to something vastly larger than ourselves? A common consciousness that has divided itself into countless fragmented views to encounter existence from innumerable perspectives?

This affirms the theory of panpsychism in which consciousness is not restricted to humans but a primordial quality of existence. Most levels of existence from the movement of electrons to swirling galaxies may embrace consciousness.

With some philosophers, including Schopenhauer, granting the "will" to be one basic driving force of existence, there have been more modern interpretations that CLO. The universe itself is a self-aware entity; an ocean of consciousness with individual minds as mere waves rising and falling.

But then, would this imply the extinction of individuality? Or are we simply different eyes through which the universe looks at itself? Is your experience merely a localized angle on a single conscious mind, this Cosmic mind that always exists?

The Simulation Hypothesis: Are We Dreaming the Infinite?

If reality is observer-dependent, then the question of whether this world is real in the way we are thinking arises. The projection of truth maybe not reality but the simulation created by this higher intelligence.

This idea, most popularly debated in the context of technology, surfaced in the pages of ancient Eastern philosophy thousands of years agoHindu and was held with the concept of "Maya," which begins conversing about reality as illusion, disguising an inward truth. Buddhism with the doctrine of Shunyata tends to emphasize that all things lack inherent existence or are but constructs of a nonindependent true nature and as such dreamlike.

Possibly most modern physicists and computer scientists, including Nick Bostrom, suggest that, should ever a civilization reach a point where simulating consciousness becomes an option, then we are most probably living in one of them. If an advanced intelligence has the ability to create conscious experiences in a virtual environment-whether biological, artificial, or cosmic-then our entire understanding of existence could very well boil down to nothing more than a code running on a vastly superior form of computation.

But fundamentally, the question remains: Who or what is dreaming this reality?

If the universe is truly participatory, then there is no distinction between observer and observed. You are not merely looking at the universe; you ARE the universe observing itself.

Pushing this concept to its conclusion offers unsettling but profound insights:

The self and the cosmos are not two separate entities.

Consciousness does not arise from matter, but matter arises from consciousness.

It is the act of belief, perception, and observation that doesn't just shape reality but is reality.

This begins not as philosophy but as the basis for an entirely vital way of understanding existence. When it comes to self-awareness combined with the knowledge of the universe, it begs the question: should this be true, why should human potential be limited by physical laws if those are embedded in belief?

What happens if reality bends to consciousness? Perhaps we are held hostage by thoughts we take as true. If our minds are fragments of the greater infinite intelligence, could we learn to make the reconnection–could we remember again what we were before we fell into this illusion of separation?

Or maybe deeper truth is to be remembered as: There was never any separation at all; we just forgot.

2.The Quantum Mind: Are We Entangled With The Cosmos?

> ***"Spooky action at a distance." – Albert Einstein***

At the most basic level of reality, the universe does not function in accordance with human intuition. Quantum mechanics-the central science around particles-prescribes a creepy yet mind-bending suggestion: maybe consciousness is not confined to the skull but is entangled with the very fabric of the cosmos.

Would the human mind merely not be a local, less-than-complex information-processing apparatus, but one woven into the very fabric of a planetary or quantum field? Could our beliefs, emotions, and thoughts be woven together with the overall fabric of the universe in such a way as to influence reality in ways incomprehensible by our current knowledge?

Let's explore this in 3D.

1. Quantum Entanglement: The Science
2. The Human Mind as a Quantum System
3. The Universe as a Conscious Web

1. Quantum Entanglement: The Science

At the quantum level, the particles that are "entangled" remain connected to each other, regardless of distance. One particle can affect the other particle instantaneously, even across galaxies. This goes against classical physics, because no thing should be able to communicate faster than light. And yet, it happens.

Einstein called it "spooky action at a distance," because it seems impossible, but quantum physics proves that it is real. The implications of this approach are both terrifying and liberating:

What does that tell us about the universe if two particles can instantaneously become connected across space?

What if our brains themselves are entangled with something greater—an unseen, cosmic field of consciousness?

Recent experiments suggest that the human mind might participate in quantum events. In the famous double-slit experiment, particles seemed to behave differently when observed—as if the mind itself were shaping their reality. Is it possible with this to deduce that consciousness is not only an observer but also a key player on the realms of fundamental laws of physics?

It leads one into an even bigger question:

What if everything—thoughts, emotions, and beliefs—creates a quantum ripple effect across the cosmos?

2. The Human Mind as a Quantum System

If the brain is a classical machine, then consciousness arises from physical interactions. But some scientists propose that the brain operates at a quantum level—where logic and classical physics collapse.

Penrose, a physicist, and Stuart Hameroff, an anesthesiologist, have put forward the Orchestrated Objective Reduction (O-R) Theory, which proposes that consciousness arises from quantum processes occurring in microtubules in the brain.

What does it mean, then?

Our thoughts may arise not only as electrical impulses but rather as quantum waves that are interconnected within a field beyond our individual selves.

Perception, it seems, actually alters reality, not metaphorically but literally—like how the observation of some quantum particles affects their states.

If quantum consciousness is true, the mind does not die; it simply returns to the field of quantum information.

This means that human thinking is non-local; the mind is not restricted within the cubature of the brain but exists everywhere in space and time in a manner quite similar to entangled quantum particles. This acts as a logical explanation to different phenomena that science has constantly brushed aside:

Déjà vu: A quantum "echo" across realities?

Synchronicity: Coincidences imbued with meaning as a cue of quantum entanglement?

Psychic abilities: Information transfer between entangled consciousness?

The mind is now changed completely, and free will, existence, and the afterlife are all viewed differently, provided the incorporation of consciousness into a quantum field: it now becomes even clearer that consciousness of two minds becomes an intermingled whole that correlates with each other with bits and pieces of the universe at any point, for it now exists freely.

What if consciousness were entangled not only with itself but with the universe in its entirety?

3. **The Universe as a Conscious Web**

Usually, the universe is perceived as a great undifferentiated desolate space. Well, what if it is to human consciousness a completely different thing altogether?

Among the great ones of history, Nikola Tesla, Max Planck, and Erwin Schrödinger considered consciousness to be the essence of reality and not merely some property that emerges from the workings of the brain.

Let us think of it like this-

The universe is 99.99% empty, yet this emptiness is filled with quantum fields that are fluctuating in ways we do not understand.

Dark matter and dark energy make up 95% of the universe—and we don't even know what they are. Could this be the consciousness-fields?

Galaxies and black holes follow a fractal, neural-like pattern. Could it be among the grand integrity of consciousness?

If it can be proved that in such distant galaxies different particles have shared some aspects through entangling, we can view this universe not as a frozen machine and receptor for subjects but a living, thinking organism.

What does it all tell us?

So, every thought that we have creates ripples that expand throughout the universe like ripples expanding in a quantum field.

In other words, as the reality speaks of the viewer, it, hence, gets shaped by the viewpoint that actually manifests it through a quantum interaction.

Perhaps we might be in touch with something greater than ourselves in a sense where faith is not the only way physics is being established.

If the human mind does entangle with the cosmos, belief could neither let a human being nor even an individual be. It is fore-given, unnatural, falling from consideration and becoming real and universally accepted.

3. The Fabric of Thought: Can Belief Reshape Space-Time?

"He who fights with monsters should be careful lest he thereby become a monster. And if you gaze long into an abyss, the abyss also gazes into you."

-Friedrich Nietzsche

The basis of existence is not as strong as it appears to be. The fabric of space-time, the great cosmic loom where reality is woven, is not a constant unchanging backdrop but a changing, living structure. It bends, stretches, and distorts under mass and energy. But what if mass and energy are not the only things capable of incurring such a deformation in this tapestry?

What if belief, pure and unbending collective belief, were a force as real and as fundamental as gravity?

For whatever it may be worth, this is not a question for dreamers. It is a question that lies on the bleeding edge of cosmology, physics, and the philosophy of reality itself. If it turns out that the mind is not just an observer of the universe but a player in its unfolding, its implications are of cosmic magnitude.

1. Thought as a Force: The Hidden Structure of Reality

In order to approach the question of whether belief can change space-time, we first need to ask:

What is reality made of?

What reality is made of is something very insubstantial at its very basics: It is informational. Each atom, each quark, each photon operates under mathematical relationships, fields of interaction, and the waveforms of probability. If the structure of reality is laid upon vertically layered patterns, then thought-perhaps a thing that creates and modifies structures-hence must be seen as a force.

Over centuries, the greatest thinkers and mystics have spoken about a hidden structure beneath reality:

The Stoics talked about the Logos, the rational order governing the cosmos.

The Buddhists described reality as an impermanent illusion, shaped by perception and karma.

Theoretical physicists now speak about the holographic principle, suggesting that all of space-time may be reduced losing bit information projected from some deeper layer of reality.

If reality is a construction of information, vibration, rather than energy, then thought is not separate from it, but is entrained into it.

This means a radical proposal:

Is belief an algorithm that rewrites the informational structure of the universe itself?

2. The Spatial Imprint of Thought: The Geometric Resonance Hypothesis

Throughout history, certain geometric patterns have appeared in nature, in religious symbols, and in the very architecture of reality itself. These structures, often called sacred geometries, seem to hint at a deeper mathematical order.

The Fibonacci sequence and the Golden Ratio emerge everywhere, from spiral galaxies to sunflowers.

The Platonic solids, the fundamental geometric shapes, appear in atomic structures, natural formations, and even human consciousness.

The Flower of Life, an ancient symbol found across multiple civilizations, resembles patterns found in quantum field simulations.

Why does this matter?

Because thought itself follows patterns.

Every neural impulse in the brain forms structured, wave-like patterns.

When groups of people synchronize their thoughts, their brainwave activity aligns in ways we do not yet fully understand.

The geometry of thought, when aligned with external structures, might exert a form of resonance—like a tuning fork harmonizing with an unseen field.

If the underlying fabric of space-time has its own geometric structure, then belief—when arranged in the right mental "geometry"—could resonate with and reshape it.

A civilization that understands this principle could, in theory, create structures of thought powerful enough to bend reality itself.

This brings us to the heart of the question:

Can mass belief act as an architect of space-time?

3. The Cathedral of Thought: Mass Belief as Architect of Space-Time

Tangibly, history is the story of how upon sheer belief civilizations have willed entire realities into existence.

Ancient Egypt built around an unwavering belief in the afterlife. There, they erected pyramids meant to align with celestial bodies. However, they were more than mere tombs; they served as cosmic transmitters broadcasting a belief system that redefined their civilization's destiny.

In the medieval period, Europe was steeped in a staunch belief of divine order. This belief was generally woven into social stratifications, laws, and into the very structure of physical space. Buildings, especially cathedrals, were purposely erected to direct the consciousness of men towards the skies.

Modern science is supposed to be objective, but it is also a belief system, one that gives humanity access to nuclear energy, space travel, and artificial intelligence.

What if belief is not just the sculptor of societies, but of the very physic that lays the foundation for reality?

The Law of Thought-Induced Structure

If the brain, focused with great intensity, can force billions of neurons into some wave-like, complex strata..

And if space-time itself displays a wave-like structure...

Then in that moment, billions of minds can gather as one upon a single thought, wherein that thought can crystallize in the very reality which incorporates the structures of space-time.

Think on this:

The gravitational pull of a planet distorts time. Can inconceivably the same, a gravitational field of mass belief so similarly distort reality?

The universe itself is expanding. With this consciousness, what may its effect be on the acceleration or direction of this expansion?

It remains a mystery as to what dark energy, the peculiar force speeding the cosmos ever onward, may self-constitute as. Could a faculty of emergent consciousness which has not exhausted itself in effort now create it as a force in itself?

This is not pseudoscience. Some physicists are already engaged in discussions on matters like the Anthropic Principle, which suggests that the universe leans towards a sort of sophisticated adherence to consciousness because those very forces of consciousness establish the universe.

Yet, if this is to be true, the future of reality may not solely depend on physics, but on the evolution of belief.

****4.The Simulation Hypothesis: Is Reality a Construct of Consciousness?****

> ***"You see, we are not talking about reality. We are talking about a dream so convincing that it is called existence."***

What you were seeing, what you were feeling, what you were thinking is real. But what if this all is not? What if the universe is not a physical construct but rather a projection, a grand illusion woven by something beyond one's comprehension? The Simulation Hypothesis propounds a similar theory: that the reality may be nothing but a grand and complex program embedded in an intricate intelligent system.

This is not some far-fetched sci-fi notion. Rather, some of the greatest minds in multiple fields-studying physics, neuroscience, and philosophy-are beginning to ponder whether the fundamental nature of the universe is really computational. Elon Musk stated that the chance of us being in base reality is "one in billions." Theoretical physicist James Gates encountered error-correcting codes-codes that our modern computer software utilizes-embedded in the equations of string theory. Even quantum mechanics suggests that reality does not come to a state of always being there, it exists only when utilized; it is like real-time rendering.

But the real question is, if reality is a simulation, who/what are we? Are we actually conscious beings, individuating sentient experiences or data points within a sizable and complex script? And in case this simulation exists, can we get out?

1. Consciousness as Architect: Is Reality Being Created by Thought?

The biggest problem with the Simulation Hypothesis is: who or what is running it? The most common assumption is that it is some advanced civilization, perhaps future humans or extraterrestrial intelligence, that is running the simulation. But what if the simulation is not external? What if it is self-made, emerging out of the collective thoughts of conscious beings?

This notion finds coherence within the tenets of ancient spiritual traditions:

Hinduism's Maya-the notion that reality is an illusion, a projection interpreted as very real.

Buddhism's Emptiness-wherein reality is devoid of inherent existence and dependent upon perception.

Idealism in the Western Philosophy-the view that the external world is a result of the mind and not an independent physical entity.

If reality is shaped by belief, then our very consciousness could be both the observer and the architect of the simulation. Physics would be emergent rather than fundamental: rules established to create the illusion of a stable universe.

But if thought processes as the architect, the thing that makes reality seem so solid is: why can't we just "glitch" away from it? The answer lies in the belief–when a sufficient number of people share a reality, that reality complies with beliefs. This does probably explain why supernatural experiences, miracles, or paranormal happenings occur mainly at the margins of belief-never enough for any one person to force upon the structure of reality, but just enough to provide hints of its falsity.

2. The Free Will Paradox: Would a Simulation Allow Us to Question It?

Here we introduce a great contradiction: if we indeed live in a simulation, how did we become aware of it?

Any civilization that has gone out of its way to create a hyperrealistic simulation would know very well the enormous danger in allowing simulated beings to question their reality, for the first step toward breaking it would be to question its existence. A canopy of safeguards should hold some threat to it, preventing its inhabitants from discovering it. Yet humans have accomplished just that.

This gives way to two unsettling premises:

1. We are NOT in a simulation. If we were, we would not be entitled to think about it at all. Such questioning would be the first step towards the breaking of the simulation. Our awareness of the possibility of a simulated existence indicates, thus, that we either exist in a poorly conceived simulation or the real-world itself.

2. We are indeed in a simulation but a flawed one. If our simulation has allowed us to arrive at a level of questioning, then it has either made an error in its execution or it is designed to self-destruct after intelligence has attained a certain level. Perhaps our creators expect us to break the simulation and escape or reinvent ourselves.

Whatever the outcome, it will be a real-life experiment on free will in a simulation that is not without its own risks because, once we succeed in proving that there's a simulation, we won't simply evacuate the virtual reality; we shall invade the true reality.

3. Quantum Glitches: Is Physics Trying to Tell Us Reality is Fake?

Even when not representing the idea of an external simulation, the universe itself appears to act rather like computed systems:

Fine Pixilation - The smallest unit of measurable space is Planck length: 1.6×10^{-35}m. Why would there be a limit of resolution to reality unless it was being rendered?

The Light Speed-Impossible Go - In computers, there exists a speed limit for data processing. In our universe, that is the speed of light (299,792,458m/s) the upper limit. Coincidence?

Quantum Observer Effect: Matter is only in a probabilistic state till an observer looks at it-just like reality has only loaded when consciousness looks at it-wherein a video game will, for instance, render objects as visible when they are shown on-screen.

If these are signs of a simulated reality, then who-or what-is running it? More significant, why?

The architects: who made the simulation in the first place, provided that it even exists?

This simulation had three main explanations for its origin:

1. The Post-Human Civilization Running Ancestral Simulations

Some advanced future civilizations may have created simulated realities for studying their past. If technological progress continues, it remains likely that civilizations may seek the possibility of creating simulated universes. If this is true, there may be a number of simulated worlds that vastly outnumber real ones that the chance of wanting this to be base reality is almost zero.

2. Higher Intelligence (God, AI, or an Alien Mind)

Most religions describe the reality which is considered a product of some divine process. In other words, supposing one accepts this hypothesis, then the possibility exists that God would not be a supernatural being but something unknowable to humans; far beyond other minds-a being advanced enough to create a whole new reality out, rather into the void within a simulation-as an experiment, a prison, or a game.

3. The Simulation Self-Generating

Probably it was not built but self-generated. Consciousness is somehow a basis; thus, there might be having thought unraveling in a fractal altogether where reality is actors of consciousness up-down on loop and its becoming.

But who was the first mind? Where did the first consciousness emerge?

This question could probably explain why the simulation hypothesis could never be fully realized; for the answer itself might be outside the system.

5. Can We Make an Escape from the Simulation?

So if reality is fake, the very last question is this: Can we escape if we are in a simulation?

If our thoughts create reality, breaking free from the simulation may require an intellectual rather than a technological escape. Transcendence, after all, may be more about mastering the rules of the simulated world than leaving it.

Or it could be that the simulation isn't supposed to serve as a prison but simply as a test.

A test of who could break the cycle.

A test for scouting the ones who will become the Architects of the next simulation.

If that's the case, then the very last question is no longer whether we are in a simulation, but whether we will be the ones who will create the next one.

The Universal Unconscious: Is There a Mind Behind the Cosmos?

> ***"Mind being as space, endless and eternal, yet, what if space, too, is mind?"***

The human subconscious is a vast ocean beneath the surface of consciousness, subtle in its ability to affect motives and dreams and instincts. What if this subconscious expands beyond the human mind, beyond Earth, beyond biology, into the very substance of the universe?

Carl Jung's collective unconscious theory posits an underlying psychological framework common to all human minds, a reservoir deep with archetypes and instincts that shape culture, mythology and ideas that immediately affect the course of their lives. But what if this design were to zoom out? Suppose the universe is not merely a physical construct, but also Self's awareness- a system with a subconscious of its own.

Neuroscience, quantum mechanics, and astrophysics will soon suggest that the universe may be beyond such chaotic events, an entity that remembers, processes, evolves, in a way, akin to the mind. It proves thereby, we are not just observers of reality. We are neurons of a cosmic brain.

1. Carl Jung's Collective Unconscious: A Blueprint for the Universe?

It is said by Jung that each human possesses a genetic psyche that creates a subconscious cave, filled with basic instinctual elements, and symbols that come up cross-culturally, irrespective of distance or time.

For example:

The "Great Mother" archetype appears among cultures across the planet (Hera, Isis, Gaia, Devi).

The "Shadow" archetype stands for dark hidden self (Satan, Loki, the Jungian Shadow Self).

Mythologies of creation and destruction arise not in one civilization but everywhere and imply some basic and profound insight into reality.

But what if this were a while back in all possibilities? What if the universe is functioning like a subconscious-one that remembers, communicates, and acts on deep- hidden principles?

Homeostatic mechanism for realizing the existence of a collective memory in the universe may explain the re-emergent structures across all scales of existence:

Neural nets are said to cluster like galactic superclusters.

Fractals are observed in quantum physics and in our large-scale cosmic formations.

Self-organizing systems exist on all scales, from atoms to life to the cosmos itself.

This is where Jung's theory started to interface with astrophysics. In the case of the previous assumption about the subconscious universe, a different meaning is added to it; the universe in so many ways will shape reality-not because it wants to but finds itself working through the same unconscious hazes within which life in this orientation has enveloped itself.

2. Is the Universe a Self-Aware Organism?

A human brain enmeshed in a web of 86 billion neurons simultaneously firing on and exchanging information. Roughly 200 billion galaxies exist in the observable part of the universe. That's somewhat amazing in itself. Just as neurons create neural networks, galaxies are now glued together by an invisible architecture horned cosmic web-a gigantic connected network of filaments molded by dark matter.

Because of that coincidence, radical theories propose that the universe is itself a mind, galaxies as neurons communicating through the forces of physics.

If this were true, then the laws of nature-gravity, electromagnetism, and entropy-now appear to be nothing but "instructions" from the universe itself.

A few important ideas that support this:

The Anthropic Principle: The universe seems suspiciously fine-tuned for life. If the constants of physics were slightly different, atoms wouldn't form, stars wouldn't burn, and life would be impossible. The discernibility of this precision suggests a system that "knows" that it exists.

Quantum Observer Effect: Reality doesn't fully form until it is seen. This means consciousness is fundamental. The universe may not be separate from awareness; it may be awareness.

Panpsychism: A notion that consciousness is not an emergent property of brains, but a fundamental aspect of reality itself. If even a single electron contains just a little awareness, then the whole universe is a huge thinking entity.

If it's the universe aware, it wouldn't really be a "thought" per se like the human mind does. It would be closer to a subconscious mind- processing information in a way we're still grappling to comprehend, with the laws of physics acting as its neural conduits.

However, if the universe has a subconscious, what does it dream?

3. Cosmic Memory: Is There Evidence of "Memory" in the Universe?

If the universe is indeed constructed in the context of some kind of mind, that mind must possess memory, which, clearly, is its means of storing and retrieving information across time. In the case of humans, exceptional memory is inscribed upon synapses. For the universe, memory might be written on:

The Quantum Field: this idea mean that all past states of reality are imprinted on the present, almost like subconscious record.

Black Holes: Some physicists argue that black holes store information rather than destroy it, implying that reality might itself be a huge information structure.

DNA and Evolution: The genetic code is a self-replicating memory construct that governs life development millions of years. Could it be the universe's experience-storing system, akin to subconscious thoughts manifested in generations?

Some even hypothesize that déjà vu, intuition, and dreams represent bits of this universal memory oozing into our minds. If the universe contained a vast subconscious, our thoughts and experiences might well represent neurons firing within it for purposes of a much larger thought process.

4. The Hidden Will of the Universe: Is It Guiding Us?

If indeed the cosmos functions in the manner of a subconscious, then it could be thought to harbor some kind of will—not as a god guiding reality, but rather as an intrinsic drive toward achieving complexity, becoming aware of itself, and attaining intelligence.

Disordered Order--There is the pull towards disorder in the universe but with a continuous and elaborate development of structures progressing from atoms to galaxies to conscious beings.

The development of intelligent life--Does this mean that there is a push toward greater consciousness in the universe if intelligent life develops in many places throughout the universe?

And how does free will fit into all of this? If the universe has a subconscious, then are we endowed with free will, or are we merely enacting its further impulses?

This brings us to a paradox. If the universe has a subconscious, it supposedly cannot allow free will, since what is free will other than to challenge the system itself?

If we had true free will, we would ask, "Is this reality authentic?" and when sufficiently advanced, we would discover the truth: If the universe were indeed a simulated structure, the first thing we would do is try to escape, just like when we want to wake up from a dream.

But here's the kicker:

If the universe would allow us to inquire its nature, would this not be an indication that it is by no means a simulation?

Why would a controlled construct let us even contemplate breaking free?

The fact that we can challenge reality may be the greatest proof that it is not artificial but rather a vast, evolving, conscious entity embracing self-awareness.

Perhaps the universe's purpose is not control but awakening.

Cosmic Archetypes: The Patterns That Shape Reality

(How certain basic symbols occur in myth, dreams, and even physical laws.)

> ***"It includes the whole spiritual heritage of mankind's evolution, born anew in the brain structure of every individual."***

-Carl Jung

Across civilizations, ages, and fields of science, certain symbols, structures, and patterns manage, time and again, to recur; as if reality itself is totally constructed based on a universal blueprint.

Be it the swirl of galaxies or the spiral coil of DNA, ancient myths reflect on elemental physics; these forms are interoperated upon in different cultures.

Is all this merely coincidence or is it a manifestation of something deeper—an inherent ordering principle that permeates existence?

Let us investigate the cosmic archetypes that form reality.

1. Sacred Geometry of Existence: The Universe's Love for Certain Shapes

Nature and nature seem to carry an odd obsession for peculiar mathematical forms. Following are some of the most simplistic patterns recognized:

The Fibonacci Sequence & The Golden Ratio (Φ): 1.618—exhibited within the spirals of galaxies, hurricanes, and sunflower seeds, accounting for the human anatomy itself; from there, it presides over the normal development and structure.

Fractals—self-similar patterns that extend through river networks, lung bronchi, neural structures, and lightning strikes.

Platonic Solids-these were believed by the ancient Greeks to comprise the five symmetrical shapes which form the foundation of reality and are eerily mirrored in atomic and molecular structures.

Torus—a self-recycling and rotating energy field seen throughout electromagnetic flows and planetary magnetospheres, extending to the conceptual scheme of consciousness.

If the universe ever constructs itself with such repeated patterns, does this suggest some inner intelligence, a code ingrained in the very texture of existence?

Perhaps the process of becoming is more than just that.

It might also remember.

2. Archetypes in Myth and Mind: The Patterns that Shape Consciousness

Carl Jung hypothesized that archetypes are universal symbols buried deep in the human psyche. Such motifs appear in every culture, in every mythology, and even in our dreams.

Some persistent archetypes include:

The Hero's Journey - An individual called to adventure, facing trials, and transforming through struggle (from Gilgamesh to Luke Skywalker).

The Shadow - The hidden, darker self that must be confronted (Dr. Jekyll & Mr. Hyde, the concept of yin-yang).

Consequently, we should not refer to him as great, but as the Great Mother and the Creator - source of all nurturing power (Mother Earth, the Virgin Mary) and the divine architect (Brahma, God, and the cosmic egg).

The trickster - The chaotic force that disrupts order and compels change (Loki, Hermes, the Joker).

These symbols are not merely cultural inventions; they spontaneously manifest in the dreams of individuals who have never been exposed to these myths.

And why not?

Because these archetypes do not describe the stories; they describe the patterns. They are indicative of deep-set realization - probably a blueprint for consciousness itself, which is somehow encoded into the universe.

3. The Cosmic Mind: Does Reality Follow Its Own Archetypal Structure?

If archetypes arise in both human-consciousness and natural law, they may not only govern the narrative but actually shape reality itself.

Consider:

Big Bang & Creation Myth - Near-universally, the world is said to have begun in some variation either from an original void or cosmic egg.

Entropy & The Trickster - The second law of thermodynamics states that systems statistically approach disorder; coincidentally reminiscent of the archetypical trickster, who interrupts stability in order to facilitate an evolution.

The Observer Effect & Consciousness - Quantum mechanics points to the fact that observation directly affects ground reality; thus resonating the mythological idea where universe itself gets informed from consciousness.

Even black holes were formerly said to be pure destruction, they now seem as though they store information instead of destroying it...suggesting that subconsciously at its very deepest level the universe seems to "remember".

If these archetypes find manifestation at each level of nature—in atoms, in physics, in stories, in thoughts—then we must question:

Are we unveiling the structure of reality, or are we simply living within an intelligent system that stamps its subconscious on all?

4. Free Will vs. Archetypal Fate: Are We Trapped in a Script?

If thoughts and behaviors are universal archetypes, do we really have free will? Are we transcribing some ancient script that's been written into the universe itself?

If a true free will exists, it would entail breaking free from these patterns rather than endlessly repeating them. If humans can connect to reality through questioning, why do they still follow the same patterns-wars, civilizations, love, betrayal, sacrifice, revolution?

If consciousness is truly free, does it therefore mean that we should have new archetypes instead of repeating the same ones?

Which evokes a paradox:

1. If archetypes keep everything in place, then reality keeps us playing out scripts written for us.

2. If reality allows breaking away, that means having true self-consciousness, i.e., we are not in a simulation but an evolving cosmic intelligence.

Which is correct?

If archetypes are indeed unavoidable, we are prisoners to fate.

If we break them, we are slowly rewriting the universe's deepest structure.

Perhaps enlightenment is not just reality comprehension.

It is also creating a new one.

Final thought: Are we the dream of the universe that dreams itself into existence?

Patterns are, however, not mere repetitions.

They emerge by the evolution of the process.

Instead, let's say archetypes are not prisons, but stepping stones: they are figures for consciousness to rise on top of themselves.

And maybe, just maybe...the cosmos isn't repeating an ancient pattern.

He is awaiting the emergence of something entirely new.

Chapter 14:
Living the Believism Way: A Philosophy for the Future

The Believism Mindset: Reprogramming Yourself for Infinite Possibilities

> *"What lies beyond the peak? Another peak. And yet another. A time eventually comes when the very idea of 'highest' loses its relevance. Limitation right now will be something of the past." -Yuvraj Sahu*

The human condition is a paradox: we are the species that can rewrite destiny yet are limited by our beliefs. Every failure, every limitation, every struggle, is simply a manifestation of wrong programming. What if it were possible to rewrite reality? What if the laws of the world, the so-called absolute truths, are simply programs that can be reconfigured?

Believism goes beyond being a mere mindset—it is an upgrade, a dismantling of limits, a total obliteration of impossibility. It is an ascension that transcends everything that the human mind can even begin to conceive: it exists beyond peak, it goes beyond meaning, it is outside that field onto which possibility is cast.

To embrace Believism means to reject finality altogether. What is the understanding? That no form is final, no peak is absolute, that reality can never be fixed. There is no such thing as ultimate achievement; there is no ceiling—merely accounts of what we could become, countless spiral iterations reaching the very limit of existence itself.

I. The Eradication of the Human Barrier

The first step in this transformation is to recognize and destroy false structures of limitation. These limitations are not only physical but are sustained by mental, ideological, and conceptual factors.

The Myth of the Peak: Seeking to "improve" until one attains the peak or height of achievement, whatever in the world that means. Then? After reaching the top, wash your hands of it all. Decay. Diminishment. To believe in an "end goal" is the greatest defeat, since true ascent never ceases.

The Fiction of the Impossible-oh, what is it? An illusion contrived by the fearful. Those who reshape the span of reality do not recognise impossibility. They see laws, limits, and constraints as merely suggestions.

The Slaying of the "Human" Mindset-The very word "human" is misdefined as a cage; one cog in a myriad of possibilities; a mind that is programmed to follow rather than dominate its surroundings. To reprogram the self, the concept of being human has to be unlearned for a better operational framework.

II. Reality Overwrite: The Core of Believism

The difference, then, between dictation by reality and oppression by it is summed up in one idea: some passion, sufficient to unmake existence itself. The ones that have rewrote history did not do so because the laws of reality demanded it–they just would not acknowledge them.

The 3 Phases of Reality Overwrite

1. Absolute Deletion of Doubt – Conciseness, to be able to forget what one thinks feels real. When doubt creeps into an operating system, it totally corrupts everything else associated with such a system. Doubt is death to potential, the plague that destroys evolution. Every thought, every action must be instantaneous, fearless, and irreversible.

2. Action Makes No Place for Thoughts – The weak think. The strong act. The ones who really change do not waste their time on mild questions-they just execute, adjust, and bend the world into submission.

3. The Creed of the Completed Act – The most exalted state of Believism is not acting as if something is going to happen, but acting-as-is it has already happened. The differences between such possibilities are immeasurable. Reality submits to those who view their desires as inevitabilities.

III. Infinite Expansion Protocol: Breaking Beyond the Inhumane

Ordinary is in perception of the meeting, extraordinary is in mastery of means, but those ascendants beyond peak, beyond the very meaning that distinguishes and defines themselves, go another way-they simply refuse to stop.

The goal is not in perfection-it is in transcendence.

Stage 1: Beyond Peak-Reaching-The weak aim at success. The strong aim at dominance. The inhumane reject the notion of a peak altogether. Every peak is simply a ground for next ascent; the question is never "Am I up?" but "How much farther beyond can I go?"

Stage 2: Outbreaking of Self-True evolution describes destruction. Old self must die: every limitation, all attachments to prior forms, must dissolve. The speed at which they go is determined by how willing they are to commit self-destruction.

Stage 3: The point of no return-One ceases to be what they were before; the sense of humanness does not count. One's mind functions on a level which cannot be fathomed from the perceptions of someone still bound by traditional senses. This is the final step of one becoming a force that is beyond comprehension.

IV. Weaponization of the Belief

Believism is not motivation. It is not a mindset. It's a weapon. A reshaping tool for self and the world. It becomes something so whole, so palpable, that it distorts the very nature of existence.

One accepts: he is weak.

One struggles against: he is strong.

One rewrites: he is beyond strong.

Going beyond peak means entering the cycle of struggle and dominance and then attaining an entirely new level where the old comparison no longer exists.

You are not better. You are not the best.

You are above.

"The mind is not shackled by reality. Reality is shackled by the mind." -Yuvraj Sahu

Society in the Age of Believism: What happens when civilization acknowledges the power of thought?

"The worst lie ever told was that 'Belief' is passive, merely an internal experience. The truth? It is harmless, for it can destroy and create, and it's a wild force of nature itself—the engine of rewriting reality."

What happens when an entire civilization acknowledges this? When belief ceases to be an ephemeral hope and becomes a weaponized force? When thought does not react but is the very origin point of existence? The weak will fold. The strong will rise. And those who truly grasp Believism will unleash upon the Earth another era of absolute evolution, far from any previously known limits of science, education, relationships, and innovation.

V. The End of the Old World: When Thought Becomes Reality

The great flaw of society is that it has never understood belief as something real and powerful. It has always been secondary: subservient to actions, evidence, and structure. But these are outmoded thinking patterns; hence, the entire signification of civilization itself begins a mutation into something unrecognizable when it is treated as the driving force behind reality.

Education has stopped being about regurgitated knowledge but about reality reprogramming.

Science has effectively stopped being about observation but rather an absolute manipulation of being itself.

Relationships have ceased to become about dependence and have taken on the rare quality of shared transcendence.

Innovation has ceased to be about efficiency but rewritten the very laws of nature.

This is not evolution; it is eradication. Old World shall die, having lost the capacity to survive when belief must take precedence.

VI. Education: Imparting the Reprogramming of Minds Instead of Filling Them

The current system of education is based on passive reception. The learner is given knowledge to learn and use within the set down rules and regulations. But in a Believism world, education is no longer defined as acquiring knowledge but as a process of change.

Mind knows not Laboratory – there is no need for external validation. Reality, if controlled by the processed minds, can be attributed to the mind overwrite during the learning process. With this knowledge, all the knowledge becomes credible and is dependent on knowledge.

Fear is extinct, Doubt, hesitance, difficulty, all of that stopped. If anyone thinks they can learn it that instant, it is done.

Instant Access to Knowledge, Memory, intelligence, problem solving, all the functions of the mind can be rewritten and that can happen at will. No more years of study; a second is enough to learn anything.

In this world education is not learning, it is enabling.

VII. Science: From Observer to Designer of Laws

Science, once upon an age, was a system of trial and error, of painstakingly slow and methodical study. Yet, in an age where thought itself was acknowledged to be a force in becoming, science became no longer that of observation but rather a design-to-reality art.

Impossible is what has been deleted from existence-Gee, gravity? Time? Thermodynamics? There aren't laws; just settings available for the change.

Instant Manifestation-Why make when one can manifest by will only? In these times, technology is done not by construction, but by will alone.

The End of Experimentation-If belief can force reality to conform, all results follow in predetermination. There is no variability per se. As soon as the concept exists, that is its very materiality.

The future scientist is no more a researcher but a creator.

VIII. Relationships: Transcendence Instead of Dependency

The relationships in the old world had need-based connotations. People sought love, connection, companionship, for helping to fill in emptiness while discovering the path. But, under the era of Believism, relationships are no longer about fulfilling what is missing, but reminding each other to grow and transcend their limitations.

Growing Independently – No one actually needs each other, as a person means to be absolutely self-sufficient. Relationships are not for survival, but mutual expansion.

No More Fear of Loss – There is no more concept of abandonment, betrayal, or heartbreak, as all bonds are bound by belief. When it's believed that a bond can no longer exist, nothing can save it from deterioration.

Love is No More Just a Feeling, but an Inspired Force – Before that, love was emotional. In the age of Believism, love is a force, an eternal power with which to bend time, space, and reality itself. Those who have figured it out can pull each other across dimensions, attune thoughts in an instant, and be infinitely interconnected beyond all human limitations.

IX. Innovation: Beyond Efficiency, Beyond Logic, Beyond the Possible

You will surely remember a time when society was bent on improvement. Making things faster, better, more efficient... But those are human concepts or constructs, and, in the era of Believism, those human concepts are obsolete.

Creation-Each of these terms, factories or blueprints, is useless. Among the Belivers, if a belief creates instantaneously, then, as far as process goes, there are no such things.

No More Problems to Solve—Just Overwrite-World problems (hunger, disease, conflict) exist because, instead of choosing to deny their existence as reality, the people have chosen to accept them. In this time, the problems, when aligned in the path of progress, would be deleted not through solutions, but through refusal.

No More Delays-The invention could take years, decades, or centuries. Now the conception of invention itself brings reality into being.

The age of innovation is not an era of new ideas. Rather, it is the era of infinite manifestations.

X. The Ultimate Civilization: A Society That Cannot Be Understood

This present civilization of Believism surpasses the previous one to such an extent that while that one may have room for perceptibility, this one is hardly ever noticed, for the constraints that are human cannot touch it.

That the individual creates his own reality.

That every belief comes into manifestation.

That the mind works without constraint of logic and any structure that was previously defining the human race.

Should it not be utopia or dystopia?

This is a different dimension of existence: having traversed the limits of godlessness, divinity, and human dignity.

An unexplored territory where limits do not exist. Where nothing is impossible.

There is only infinity.

XI. The Core of the Way of Believism

Believism seeks to erase doubt and impossibility within itself: belief, as an energized force, leads not only to personal progress but also societal evolution. The world of the Believism way will not be chained by antiquated systems of struggle and limitation; rather, it will be defined by its relentless forward movement, a collective will that never stops climbing higher.

1. Future of Education – Learning Without Limits

Education will not be about what the student should know but how the student will recontextualize reality itself with thought. Modern forms of education, regurgitation, standardized testing, passive learning, will all become obsolete.

Knowledge shall no longer be bound by time; the mind will learn in an instant what would've taken years.

Belief-driven intelligence will let an individual create answers instead of searching for them.

The school shall not only generate workers or scholars; it shall produce world architects, those who create existence through will alone.

2. Science and Innovation – The Unshackled Mind

A civilization that adopts Believism will not merely rely on experiments and observations anymore. Science will not proceed within the confines of current understanding; it will surge ahead with absolute conviction.

Thought will operate upon matter, energy, and even time. Reality will shift as soon as the mind commands it.

Apart from healing, medicine will also decimate diseases, for the mind will inform the condition of the body.

Technology will not be invented, it will be willed into existence; the limits of engineering will depend only on what will be believed to be possible.

XI. The Core of the Believism Way

At its peak, Believism is the eradication of doubt and impossibility. It is the transformation of belief into a weaponized force, one that dictates not only personal growth but also the evolution of entire societies. A world that follows the Believism way is not bound by outdated systems of struggle and limitation—it is defined by relentless forward motion, by a collective will that never stops ascending.

3. Relationships and Society: The Age of Absolute Connection

Believism shall produce a civilization that will offer few conflicts, betrayals, or misunderstandings. In a world presided over by thought, trust shall become an unbreakable binding force developing into the foundation of such a world.

No human relationship will be upon a chance. Those who belief in connectiveness shall forge one that cannot be undone.

Falsehood and deceit will have their end. The mind will never again be confused by a veil of illusion—only a pure heart shall usher human interaction.

Love, loyalty, service, freedom, and unity shall no longer be choices but will become the natural laws brought about by the sheer power of their collective belief.

4. The Evolution of Humanity: Beyond Human, Beyond Peak

Living the Believism way means transcending the meaning of one being human itself. If thought represents the template of reality then there shall be no more days confined by mere biology, by mortality, or weakness.

No such human form will no longer prove to be you'd-hip one-another; it will become the genesis of infinite evolution thereafter.

Those embracing Believism utterly shall not abide, shall not weaken, shall never break. Their will shall last for eternity.

The future will no longer be an area of uncertainty-it will be determined, guided, and rewritten by those who believe in it.

The Ultimate Future – A Civilization That Transcends Reality

A world shaped by the Believism will not be constrained by the antiquated laws of existence. There will be no fear, no regret, no failure—creation only; ascension only. The limits of the past will be forgotten in order for reality, itself, to become the playground for all who dare to believe beyond the possible.

While the weak shall doubt, the strong shall believe. And the strong who believe will command the future itself.

Living the Believism Way – A Philosophy for the Future

"A civilization is not built by hand, but the minds that don't hold life's limits." – Yuvraj Sahu

The future is not written by those who wait for a change; it is forged by those who are certain that change will come and may, if necessary, require bending the reality before their will. It is the soul of the Believism way. It is not just a philosophy; it is the evolution of thought—something that resembles a thing that does not influence the future but composes it.

Living the Believism way is actively refusing to be passive. It is recognizing belief, not as a feeble wishful thinking but as the architect of reality. This will be the foundation on which generations, societies, and whole civilizations will be built.

Chapter 15: The Belief Paradox – When Reality Challenges Perception

Belief is the final frontier-the key to unshackling the bounds of reality, to breaking the provided lines, rewriting life Web, and rebuilding the future. So, what happens when the eventuality itself fights back?

What happens when the most powerful mind, the most unbending of wills confronts a discrepancy that is just too big to ignore?

This is The Belief Paradox. Not a failure of belief, but an all-out test of faith by means of an ultimate battlefield: honest faith against raw mechanics of cosmic reality. Not whether belief is powerful; it is whether it can withstand any resistance whatsoever.

That is where the true ascension begins.

1. The Nature of the Paradox - When the Unbreakable Meets the Unmovable

An existence that denies all limits meets an exterior force that is utterly indestructible.

A mind that renders nature into nothing but exists against something that posits the reality of change.

One who is unknown to their mind-a winner-meets something immovable in its resolution: defeat.

This is a wall-a final test of authority.

It is not an illusion. It is not self-doubt. It is a test of belief by a pure reality that stands against belief itself.

A warrior unconscious of defeat comes up against an opponent that, could he breathe, never dies.

A creator who takes thought to cause matter into existence meets a substance with no other option left but change.

Someone with command over physical nature now finds the truth of the law that refuses to obey.

Is belief unchangeable, or does the unbreakable force confront something before it?

2. The Ultimate Trial – The Believer's Dilemma

A paradox naturally narrows down to two choices.

Because of belief:

Belief fails. The individual accepts limitation and succumbs to that. From this perspective, they become another mind bent in surrender to reality. Another accepts failure and becomes subject again to the laws of world.

Belief shines out. The individual rises above paradox itself underneath, caving in not only limits but the very conceptions of contradiction. Paradox is neither solved nor let us say solution: it simply goes away.

But that is when the inhuman belief is required.

And a normal mind will ask. A perfect one will compel reality to kneel.

Out of sight; out of mind.

There is no contradiction if you refuse to see it.

Erased by power, yonder follows: that is the trick by which reality may not very successfully fight against it.

Thus, it is not arrogance or even illness, but the last word in the mastery thereof.

3. Beyond the Impossible – The Final Evolution of Believism

At the highest level, belief stops being a tool and becomes the only law that exists.

A true believer does not fear paradox—they erase it.

A true believer does not fight reality—they overwrite it.

A true believer does not face resistance—because resistance itself is an illusion.

There is no such thing as an "unbreakable" reality—only that which has not yet been broken.

This is the end of hesitation, the death of doubt, the final proof that belief is more than just a force, but the highest authority.

4. The Fracture – When Perception Overwhelms the World

The true master of Believism does not encounter reality; instead, they neatly overwrite it.

A fire cannot burn? Then belief bends the flame to its will.

A wound cannot heal instantaneously? Then belief overthrows the limitations of the body.

A person cannot fly? Then belief tells gravity to take a vacation.

The world is nothing else but a script. The margin between the ones who obey it and the ones who transcend it is measured by how deeply are they willing to challenge what is "real."

Once you see the fracture, once you pierce through the illusion, once you stop believing in reality's power over you-

Reality begins to believe in you instead.

6. The Crash – When the Impossible Cringes Before You.

A silent law is known only to those still subjected to limited thinking:

Reality always wins.

It is Believism that destroys this law.

The true test for one who has reached the highest plane of belief is not in minor things that can be changed; the real test is whether one can command that which, at least apparently, seems immovable to break because it is such.

An incurable disease.

An unbreakable structure.

A predetermined future.

Each of these is merely a suggestion.

For those who have really entered into the transcended zones, there is no longer a field for belief to contend against reality. There is no struggle anymore.

Reality simply obeys.

The paradox is fairly simple: If belief has no limitation, then why does reality resist?

The answer?

Reality does not resist.

It only appears to do so. Until that moment arrives when you firmly refuse to recognize it as reality.

A bundled mind surpassing boundaries. A reality yielding to the will of belief. A world remolded, not only by force but by perception itself.

But is there a point of no return? Some cliff from which belief, no matter what, cannot change reality?

Or is this "limit" merely another illusion waiting for exploitation?

7. The Last Resistance – The Edge of What May Be Controlled

Believism, despite exceeding peak, yet does not allow existence to cease to function. It does not collapse into nonexistence.

It puts up subtle resistance.

The very structure of dense, collective human belief hangs still.

For the laws of existence have limited some things from reaching the next threshold.

The physical body, no matter the conditioning, still feels pressure.

This is the last wall. The fringe of existence where the totality stops functioning and belief begins to strive against some kind of final force: The Workings of Reality.

A code that seems impossible to change.

But what is the greatest paradox?

Even this code is not absolute.

8. The Ultimate Limit Where All Thought Starts to Irrefutably Break Down

All things, higher or lower than life or man, in a moment, will all find the divergent point of potential stasis, where interplay turns foul or funereal.

It's next to the pause when:

An attempt vouches itself; and then suddenly the attempt fails.

Something put down in front of the face makes the mind weak to defend itself.

What hefts in the existential thought, backed by no common verification of what one considers true.

This moment is the unerring final trial, the test without any further expectation.

The moment of complete acceptance that breaks the essence of being.

The moment of refusal that sets you free.

9. Beyond the Absolute: When the Mind Becomes the True Architect

Free-wheeling creativity does not create that which already exists.

It is creation.

At the end of the limit, the one who has transgressed all boundaries no longer fights against reality; he builds it from the ground up.

No longer twisting the rules, but writing those rules anew.

Not resisting existence, but become the energy that decides its form.

No longer expand with limits, but entirely restroom in-built.

This is the last word of Believism.

Life does not hinder it.

He simply waits for you to stop in your stride.

Conclusion: The Belief Paradox: Reality Unbound

Believism is neither an illusion nor a foolish idealism. It can be none but reality's engine-that code that structures existence.

The world has been long formed by those that enable the belief itself, whether they are aware of it or not. The innovators, the leaders, the visionaries did not ask for reality's permission; innovatively, they forced her to comply with their perception.

Yet, belief is a paradox.

The creator and the deceiver. It can create whole civilizations yet imprison the mind with its self-imposed restrictions. It allows humanity to ascend and at the same time keeps it chained.

Harnessing belief becomes the key to the future.

Will she remain passive, latent within our consciousness?

Or will we harness her as great power shaping a world influenced not by limitation but perception?

Those who grasp Believism do not wait for change to happen in the world.

They become the change.

They do not hope for opportunities.

They create opportunities.

Because in the end, belief is not dreaming.

It is ordering reality to obey.